Viewing
Bali &
Lombok

Above: Legong *dancer*
Right: *models of surfboards*

Sean Sheehan's Bali & Lombok

Getting around

Bemos are minibuses that travel fixed routes and can be flagged down anywhere along their route. They are very common on Bali and Lombok. *Bemos* do not display numbers, destinations or charges and the inexpensive fare is paid direct to the driver or conductor. It is best to have loose change ready and it helps to have some idea of the likely fare by enquiring at your place of accommodation. Metered taxis are everywhere in Bali; they are inexpensive, air-conditioned and most drivers are able to speak some English.

The art galleries in Ubud are a highlight of any visit to Bali

It is not difficult to eulogize Bali and Lombok, even though they are only two of over 17,000 islands that make up Indonesia. Bali is unique, not least because it is the only Hindu society in the whole of Southeast Asia. Over a million tourists now pour into the island every year and yet it is still easy to be delighted and intrigued by the Balinese way of life. The people are deeply religious, enormously talented and artistic, and possess a natural grace that will disarm even the most cynical tourist. And, just for good measure, the island is blessed with superb beaches and a warm tropical climate that endows every day with a glorious abundance of flowers and flowering shrubs, guaranteed to turn any gardener green with envy. Along with the sunshine comes an inexpensive cuisine that is well tuned to Western tastes, one more aspect of a highly creative culture. In case this picture of Bali seems too idyllic to be true, there is also Kuta, a tourist capital relentlessly catering to the materialistic whims of visitors.

To the east of Bali lies the smaller island of Lombok. The people here are mostly Muslims and the feel of the place is quite different; Lombok is a place to retreat to, a place to forget about the Western world. Between them, Bali and Lombok offer an enjoyable and beguiling mix of culture and consumerism, relaxation and escape.

Bali & Lombok's Features

Geography

Bali and Lombok are two of the smaller islands of the Indonesian archipelago, which stretches for some 5,000km between Malaysia and Australia. Bali is only 140km from east to west, 80km from north to south, while Lombok is even smaller at 80km by 70km.

Soubriquets
'Morning of the World', 'Land of a Thousand Temples' (20,000 actually), 'The Last Paradise', and 'Island of the Gods' are only some of the soubriquets reflecting the charm of Bali.

Population

Bali has 3 million inhabitants and Lombok has about 2½ million. In July and August Bali's population increases to 4 million due to the massive influx of visitors. Lombok receives 100,000 visitors annually.

Language

Bahasa Indonesia is the national language of Indonesia and is learnt in the schools. The Balinese have their own language and the Sasak inhabitants of Lombok speak Sasak. English is widely understood across Bali, but in Lombok English is spoken in tourist areas only.

Caste

The Balinese language has three forms of address depending on the caste of the person being addressed and the situational context. The choice of a first name for a Balinese child is also governed by caste and there is a surprisingly small number of names available for each caste. Ask a Balinese about this; it is a fascinating topic of conversation.

Religion

The overwhelming majority of Balinese are Hindus and, apart from a small number of people in East Java, they are the only Indonesians to follow this religion. Balinese Hinduism is a fusion of mainstream Hinduism with elements of Buddhism and animism. The majority of people in Lombok are Muslims.

Time and effort goes into creating offerings of fruit at a temple

Essence of Bali & Lombok

These islands offer the rare opportunity to witness ancient cultures living and working in a modern environment. In Bali, Hinduism is suffused with animism, the belief that the spirit world is everywhere. The countless number of temples, shrines and devout rituals, such as the tiny offerings of flower petals laid on the pavement, are only the outward signs of a spirituality that will inspire visitors.

Bali and Lombok contain a rich geographic tapestry that weaves together majestic volcanoes, lush rainforests, barren plains, rocky coastlines, sandy beaches and coral gardens.

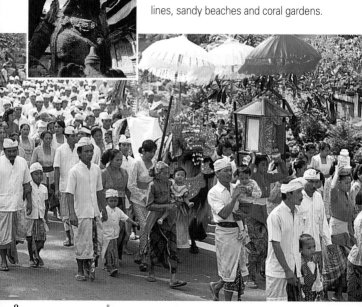

THE 10 ESSENTIALS

If you only have a short time to visit Bali and Lombok, or would like to get a complete picture of the islands, here are the essentials:

• **See at least one Balinese dance** (▶ 112) – preferably in Ubud where there is also a chance to see a rare all-women's gamelan orchestra.

• **Spend an evening in Kuta** – love it or hate it, a night of shopping and entertainment here is quite different to anywhere else (▶ 38)!

• **Spend time around Ubud** – this cultural and artistic capital (▶ 50–5) is a must for anyone interested in the arts. Seek out the paintings, traditional and modern, in Ubud's art galleries (▶ 25) and in Penestanan (▶ 61).

• **Attend a temple festival** – the tourist board issues a festival calendar, and visitors are welcome.

• **Visit a volcano** – there are plenty of volcanos on the islands to choose from: Gunung Agung (▶ 17) and Gunung Batur (▶ 18–19) in Bali, and Gunung Rinjani (▶ 83) in Lombok.

• **Watch the sun set over a temple** – Tanah Lot (▶ 47) and Uluwatu (▶ 16) are renowned for their sunsets.

• **Be inspired by the sun setting over the horizon** while you stroll along a **tropical beach** – Lovina (▶ 72–3) and the Gili Islands (▶ 21) are great spots.

• **Worship the sunshine and acquire a suntan** – but never forget you are only 143km south of the equator and the average temperature is 26°C.

• **Find time to relax and talk with the Balinese** – ask about the caste system of their names or tooth-filing ceremonies.

• **Try some snorkeling** – it is easy, safe and utterly engrossing.

Images of tranquillity, secular and religious, from Bali and Lombok

9

The Shaping of Bali & Lombok

500,000BC
During the Ice Ages, when the sea levels are lower, the land masses of Australia and South-east Asia are joined across the Indonesian archipelago, allowing the migration of the earliest animals and humans. Bali and Lombok, however, are believed to have remained separated (▶ 84).

300BC
The Bronze Age sees the development of many of the earliest settlements on Bali, while Lombok remains lost to time. In the coming centuries Indian traders introduce Hinduism to parts of the archipelago.

AD1343
Bali is colonized by a Hindu kingdom from Java and during the 16th century, when the Javanese empire loses out to Islam, Bali emerges as a place of refuge for Hindu believers. Islam bypasses Bali but not Lombok.

This sculpture from the Museum Bali was inspired by Hindu beliefs

10

1588
The Portuguese plan to erect a fort on Bali to exert command over the important spice islands but their ship sinks offshore and the surviving sailors are not allowed to leave the island. A decade later, the Dutch arrive and this time some of the Dutch sailors voluntarily decide to stay.

1846
The Dutch land their first military force on Bali, followed by another expedition two years later that leads to a fierce battle ending with the Dutch routed by the Balinese. The Europeans return in 1849 and assert their control after a number of bloody battles. The Dutch establish their head-quarters in the north of the island but local *rajas* (kings) are allowed to continue their rule.

1891
After 200 years of resisting Balinese incursions, eastern Lombok decisively throws off its Balinese overlords. Lombok, however, is ruled by the Dutch before the end of the century.

1906
The Dutch extend their control to the south of Bali by attacking Denpasar. The Balinese nobility march out defiantly and suicidally to meet the superior military technology of their enemy.

1930s
Tourists begin to arrive on Bali during the 1930s and a small but significant number of artists choose to settle here.

1941–50
The Japanese invade Indonesia in 1942 and occupy Bali without serious opposition, exposing Dutch vulnerability –

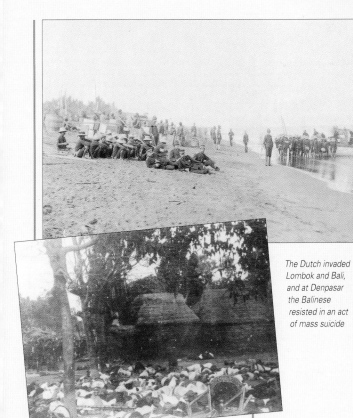

The Dutch invaded Lombok and Bali, and at Denpasar the Balinese resisted in an act of mass suicide

within days of Japan's surrender in 1945 Indonesia declares its independence. After four years of fighting the Dutch, independence (*Merdeka*, or freedom) is gained in 1949. In 1950 the Republic of Indonesia is formed, with Sukarno as president.

1960s
In 1963 Gunung Agung erupts killing thousands of Balinese and making many more homeless. In 1965 (called by Sukarno 'The year of living dangerously') General Suharto unleashes anti-communist pogroms that kill thousands more on Bali and Lombok.

Suharto becomes the nation's second president in 1968.

1990s
Bali and Lombok stay relatively calm as the nation rejects Suharto. Caretaker president B.J.Habibie is replaced in 1999 by Abdurrahman Wahid ('Gus Dur').

11

Peace & Quiet

The Bali Starling
Rothschild's mynah (*Leucopsar rothschildi*), more commonly known as the Bali starling, is now an extremely endangered species. In the mid-1960s it was first classified as in danger of extinction when the total number left in the wild was around 150. Today, there are thought to be only about 50 and breeding programs are urgently underway to try and preserve the species. The Bali starling has white wings with black tips and a striking electric-blue mask. It is Bali's one true endemic species.

The southeast of Bali is where most Balinese live and work, and is the region where the majority of visitors stay. Pockets of peace and quiet do exist and in this respect Sanur is preferable to Kuta or Nusa Dua. Candi Dasa, to the east, is a developing resort but it never becomes hectic. Not surprisingly, though, you need to go further afield to feel you are really escaping the crowds. The best balance between tranquillity and visitor comfort lies along the north coast of the island. The beach resort area of Lovina (▶ 72–3) stretches for 8km, and although it is getting busier here, there is a sense of space and openness about the place that is quite different to the beach resorts in the south. On Bali's northeastern tip, around the village of Amed (▶ 70), pleasant beachside accommodation offers visitors the opportunity to relax on Bali's forgotten corner, with its dry, almost Mediterranean climate and dramatic, rocky coast with small deserted bays. Sit in cool restaurants and enjoy great local seafood with the best views of Gunung Agung in the whole of Bali.

Bali Barat, Taman Nasional

Bali Barat National Park (▶ 56), in the northwest corner of Bali, is rich in wildlife and offers open savannah, long walks and isolation. It is the only place where you might glimpse the Bali starling in the wild, although you are more likely to spot bulbuls, orioles, sunbirds and banded pittas. The Prapat Agung walk is an excellent two-hour trail for bird-watching, while Gunung Klatakan can be climbed in about four hours by anyone seeking strenuous exercise as well as isolation.

Lombok

The island of Lombok offers the most complete escape from the hustle and bustle of towns. Tourist activity is confined to Senggigi (▶ 23) and the Gili Islands (▶ 16), but even these two places are low-key compared with most parts of Bali. The rest of the island is ripe for exploration. With your own transport, seek out deserted beaches, unspoiled stretches of coastline and small traditional villages unused to visitors – the area around Kuta (▶ 84) in the south is particularly good in this respect. For a more active retreat, consider Tetebatu (▶ 90), where the picturesque landscape can be explored on foot.

A peaceful view of Bali through palm trees (left); and the quiet of a deserted Lombok beach (above)

13

People of Bali & Lombok

Rice Paddies
One feature of Bali well worth noting is the system of irrigation used to water the terraced rice paddies. The rivers and streams cut too deep into the volcanic rock to allow for easy irrigation, so farmers have cut tunnels through the soft rock and used intricate systems of bamboo pipes to channel the water where it is needed. They are as carefully maintained today as when they were first built – some as long as 1,000 years ago.

The Balinese

Balinese society and culture pivots tightly around the family unit. The Balinese live not so much in houses, but in family compounds, a new unit attached for each new generation. Bali is renowned not for famous individuals but for its collective personality. This unique Hindu society in a predominantly Muslim nation has a way of life and set of attitudes that endears itself to all who spend time on the island. The Balinese are a genuinely friendly people who have dealt with the annual onslaught of over a million visitors with a degree of success difficult to imagine anywhere else. Balinese culture expresses itself in a number of ways. Whole villages are dedicated to painting, woodcarving or stonemasonry, and everywhere there is a profusion of natural artistic talent. The performers who faultlessly execute the intricate movements of the famous dances are rarely professionals, and the woman who brings a flask of tea to a guest in her Ubud homestay may well be a player in a *gamelan* orchestra at the weekend.

The Sasaks of Lombok

The Sasaks are the largest ethnic group in Lombok, with their own language and traditions. Unlike the Balinese, but in common with the majority of Indonesians, they are Muslims. Until well into the 1980s most Sasaks had little experience of visitors and even today most islanders' lives are unaffected by tourism.

Terraced rice paddies are irrigated by elaborate watering systems

Top Ten

Above: *Uluwatu*

Right: *painting in Ubud's Museum Neka*

1
Pura Luhur Uluwatu

This highly revered 11th-century temple is perched dramatically on a promontory above the crashing waves of the Indian Ocean.

Uluwatu temple was reputedly built in the 11th century by Mpu Kuturan, a Hindu priest from Java, and rebuilt in its present state in the 16th century by another priest, Pedanda Wawu Rauh

Its spectacular location is what makes this temple so popular with visitors. This most holy temple is balanced on the very tip of a narrow promontory some 70m above the crystal-blue sea and crashing white surf. The building would not have commanded anywhere near as much attention if it had been placed inland but its clifftop setting is magnificent. It is best seen at sunset – but be warned, this is the time when crowds suddenly appear. On arrival,

 29D1

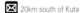 20km south of Kuta

Restaurants ($) along the road into Uluwatu

Public transport to and from Uluwatu is unreliable; use your own transport or join one of the many tours

Cheap

Pantai Suluban (► 43)

A sash must be worn

your attention is likely to be distracted by the mischievous troupe of resident monkeys. The temple carvings are very well preserved, due to the use of hard, dark-grey coral stone in construction. The *candi bentar* (split gateway) into the middle area of the temple complex is the only section that can be appreciated at close quarters because the inner part of the temple, which reaches to the cliff edge, is usually closed to visitors. From the outside, though, it is possible to view the three-tiered shrine with its thatched roofs, known as the *meru*. What makes Pura Uluwatu so holy to the Balinese is not aesthetics but its status as one of the island's sacred directional temples dedicated to the spirits of the sea. Surfing enthusiasts know the area for the surf at nearby Pantai Suluban, reached by a rough track close to the temple carpark. This beach is unsuitable for swimming but there are a number of inexpensive cafés where you can eat, drink, watch the surfing action and admire the great ocean view.

2
Gunung Agung

At 3,142m, this is Bali's highest mountain, and, with a crater summit over 500m across, it is an imposing and unforgettable sight.

The majestic sight of this volcanic mountain dominates the landscape of eastern Bali and both its physical and spiritual presence is keenly felt by the Balinese. In 1963 it erupted with such force that the top 100m were blown to pieces. The catastrophe was widely interpreted as an act of divine displeasure because the mountain has always been revered as the island's most important home for spirits. It is still regarded as the most holy place, as you will soon realise when your guide begins the climb by making an offering at a temple.

Climbing Gunung Agung takes at least five hours from nearby Besakih (the only route that reaches the very summit). Set off in the early hours of the morning in order to reach the top before dawn and before clouds set in.

Take an alternative and easier route from the town of Selat to the south of Besakih. The climb takes about three hours and stops just short of the actual summit, but the views to the east and down into the summit's crater are astonishing. Book guides through the tourist office in Besakih or in the town of Selat (no tourist office), but bring your own supplies, including a torch and some warm clothes. A successful climb does not require any experience of mountain climbing but a guide is required. You do need to be fit as there are steep areas of bare rock. Your efforts will be well rewarded once you reach the top.

29E3

Bemos run to Besakih from Klungkung and to Selat from Amlapura. Tour buses from Kuta or Ubud

65km northeast of Denpasar

Bring your own food and water if climbing the mountain

Besakih (▶ 70)

Besakih tourist office is at the car park (🕐 8–6)

A guide should be hired (at a moderate cost)

Gunung Agung is the highest mountain on Bali, home to the most important temple, at Besakih, on the island

3

Gunung Batur and Lake Batur

29E3

4km east of Penelokan

Restaurants ($) at Toya
Bungkah; Kintamani–
Penelokan main road
has restaurants ($$)
along it

Buses run from
Penelokan to Denpasar
and to Singaraja. *Bemos*
run from Penelokan to
Songan and Toya
Bungkah

Batur caldera: cheap

Penelokan (▶ 73), Pura
Ulun Danu Batur
(▶ 75), Trunyan (▶ 76)

*Lake Batur lies within the crater of
Gunung Batur, an active volcano but one
climbed annually by thousands.*

The Batur caldera was created some 30,000 years ago
when a huge volcano blew itself to pieces. What remains
now is the brooding Gunung Batur and a beautiful
crescent-shaped lake. Climbing Gunung Batur (1,717m) is
not difficult and there is even a tea shop at the summit.
This, and the crowds of people who gather before dawn at
the top, make it all seem deceptively normal – until wisps
of steam rising from fissures in the rock remind you that
this volcano is not extinct.

Scenic Lake Batur, the largest in Bali, is 3km wide and
almost three times as long. The lake, revered by the
Balinese as home to the goddess Ida Batara Dewi Ulun
Danu, is a splendid sight, whether seen from above on the
main road or approached on the winding road that twists
its way down from Penelokan. About 8km along this road
from Penelokan is Toya Bungkah, offering accommodation
and a wide range of restaurants. This is also the most
straightforward place to begin an ascent of Gunung Batur.
The climb takes less than
two hours and during the
day you don't need to take a
guide since the paths are
well trodden and easy to
follow. The first part of the
journey is through a forest,
and then it's a climb up the
rock face and a scamper

over shifting volcanic sand before a final steep stretch to the top. Consider hiring a guide if you are setting off in early morning darkness to catch the sunrise (a 4AM start is recommended). Ask your guide about having breakfast cooked on the summit.

Nearly all the towns and villages in the vicinity suffer from an over-dependence on tourism. Batur and Kintamani share an interesting temple, Pura Ulun Danu Batur, but little else besides. The lakeside village of Kedisan forms an important junction: bear left for Toya Bungkah, right for the villages of Abang and then Trunyan along the south side of the lake. The stretch of road leading to Abang is particularly picturesque and, though the road ends at Abang, there is a footpath that hugs the lake for a 4km walk to Trunyan. The other road from Kedisan that heads along the north side of the lake takes in the rather decrepit hot springs at Toya Bungkah. Continue on to the quiet village of Songan where there is a restaurant and a temple. Behind this temple a footpath allows a 15-minute walk to a vantage point on the rim of the outer crater. If you have your own transport, explore the road beyond Songan for its solitude and further views of the lake and crater rim.

Gunung Batur and Lake Batur provide a backdrop to an informal market

4
Lake Bratan

The lake is located in an ancient volcanic crater and there are opportunities for quiet, scenic walks in a cool mountain area.

✚ 29D3

✉ 48km north of Denpasar

☎ Bali Handara Kosaido Country Club: 0362-22646

🍴 Restaurants ($) in nearby Bedugul

🚌 Buses run to Bedugul from Denpasar and Singaraja

↔ Bali Botanical Gardens (► 56), Pura Ulun Danu Bratan (► 63), Taman Rekreasi Bedugul (► 64)

The pagoda-like towers (known as meru) of Pura Ulan Danu Bratan look down on Lake Bratan

There are a number of attractions around Lake Bratan that appeal to tourists and Balinese visitors but, as the area is well spread out, it rarely seems crowded. At 1,200m above sea-level, the cool air is ideal for walking and a popular short stroll is from the leisure park at Bedugul (Taman Rekreasi Bedugul) to a group of caves supposedly cleared for the Japanese during World War II. From here an easy-to-follow path leads to the summit of Gunung Catur (2,096m) where there is a small temple. Allow about three hours to make the ascent. Alternatives include hiring a canoe and paddling around the lake, or playing a round of golf at the nearby Bali Handara Kosaido Country Club, which makes the credible claim that its fast par-72 course is the only one situated inside a volcanic crater.

Far less strenuous than climbing Gunung Catur is a stroll around the southern side of Lake Buyan, 7km to the north of Lake Bratan. The nearest spot to park is in the village of Yehmas and from here it is easy to walk down to the lakeshore. There is another scenic lake to the west, Lake Tamblingan, best reached by taking the road that heads west from the village of Pucak, which is situated on the main road heading north from Lake Bratan.

5

Gili Islands

These small tropical islands offer seclusion in return for modest tourist facilities. While away the time snorkeling and enjoying the tranquillity.

These three islands – Gili Air, Gili Meno and Gili Trawangan – off the northwest coast of Lombok are becoming increasingly popular with young travelers on a tight budget. The beaches are clean, the coral is accessible, food and accommodation are inexpensive (although more upmarket places are springing up), and nightlife is simple – watching the sunset and socializing over drinks.

Gili Trawangan is the largest, liveliest and most popular of the islands, but it takes only two hours to do a complete circuit on foot (▶ 85) and most of the tourist facilities are

➕ 80A2

✉️ Off the northwest coast of Lombok

🍴 Restaurants ($) on all the islands

🛳️ From Bangsal throughout the morning; journey time averages 30 minutes

↔️ Senggigi (▶ 25), Sira (▶ 88)

concentrated along the south coast. Gili Air is the smallest, with hotels and restaurants more evenly spread out, and offers the best balance between the 'party island' atmosphere of Trawangan and the solitude of Gili Meno. Gili Meno has the best accommodation and is the most peaceful of the islands.

Snorkeling equipment is available for hire on all the Gili Islands, and scuba-diving operators on Air and Trawangan offer PADI (Professional Association of Diving Instructors) courses and facilities for qualified divers. Choose an operator with some care – compare the deals offered and ask other scuba-divers about their experiences.

Most boats leave for the islands from Bangsal. If you are based in Senggigi, consider a day trip direct from Senggigi to Gili Trawangan. Perama, the Bali bus company, runs a bus-and-boat package from Bali as well as Lombok. Between May and August try to arrive early in the morning since accommodation is occasionally overbooked.

Enjoying idyllic solitude on the Gili Islands

❓ **Perama**
✉️ Jalan Legian, Kuta, Bali ☎ 0361-751551; and ✉️ Padang Tegal, Ubud, Bali ☎ 0361-974722; and ✉️ Senggigi, Lombok ☎ 0370-93007
Trips organized by many tour agents in the town or through most hotels

6
Tirtagangga

✚ 29F3

✉ 85km from Denpasar, 20 minutes drive from Candi Dasa

🕐 Water Palace: daily 7–6

🍴 Tirta Ayu restaurant ($) inside the Water Palace grounds (► 58)

🚌 *Bemos* to Amlapura from Candi Dasa, then Amlapura to Tirtagangga

✋ Water Palace: cheap

↔ Amlapura (► 34), Pura Lempuyang Luhur (► 74)

The main attraction is the delightful Water Palace but Tirtagangga also offers cool air, beautiful countryside and opportunities for relaxing walks.

Tirtagangga comes from *Tirta* (holy water) and *Gangga* (from the Ganges) and its Water Palace was built in 1947–8 by the last raja of Amlapura. The Water Palace has been damaged more than once as a result of Gunung Agung's eruption in 1963 and an earthquake in 1979. Careful restoration work has preserved the modest grandeur of an elegant channeling system that has water spouting from the mouths of various stone demons into ornamental ponds. Besides admiring the talent of the stonemasons and architects, one can rest in the shade of the garden incorporated into the Water Palace, take a plunge into one of the two adjoining pools, or enjoy a drink and the fine view at the Tirta Ayu restaurant in the grounds of the palace.

The countryside surrounding Tirtagangga is blessed with some of the most impressive rice terraces to be found anywhere in Bali and the reasonably priced accommodation within walking distance of the palace may tempt you to stay overnight. If so, it is well worth spending a morning walking in the vicinity. With your own transport, an excursion may be made by heading north to the village of Abang, where a sign points to the right for Pura Lempuyang Luhur, 8km away. This temple is perched on top of a mountain and it takes two hours to reach the top. It's worth the effort just for the view.

Cooler temperatures around Tirtagangga enhance the charms of its Water Palace

7
Sanur

*Sanur is a laid-back beach–resort area for
discerning visitors who appreciate a little class
as well as sun and sea.*

There are three highly-developed beach resort areas in
southern Bali – Kuta, Nusa Dua and Sanur. The latter is for
those who wish to escape the excesses of Kuta while also
avoiding the stringently upmarket prices of Nusa Dua. The
beach stretches for about 4km and has the full range of
water sports – snorkeling, surfing, paddle boards,
windsurfing, water-skiing, parasailing – with the better
hotels (▶ 101) having their landscaped grounds and
swimming pools backing down close to the sea. Most of
the hotels are mid-range ones, with a few top notch
names, and a smattering of budget places.

The nightlife in Sanur doesn't pretend to compete with
Kuta but there are plenty of restaurants to suit most tastes
and budgets, a few bars, and a wide range of tourist shops
(▶ 107, 109). The street
hawkers are reasonably
discreet, which contributes to
the general air of relaxation
that characterizes Sanur.

For most of this century
Sanur has been tempting
foreigners to settle into
an expatriate life and one
artist's home has become a
museum, the Museum Le
Mayeur.

Visitors based in Sanur will
have no problems making
trips to other parts of Bali.
There are regular tourist
buses to all the popular destinations and Kuta is close
enough to reach by taxi. For
short trips from one end of
Sanur to the other there are
regular *bemos* and metered
taxis. Hiring a bicycle is also
worth considering because
the roads are flat and an early
morning cycle ride is a
wonderful way to leave the
beach behind and see the
local farmers busy in their
ricefields.

✠ 29D1

✉ 15km northeast of Kuta

🍴 A full range of
restaurants ($–$$$)
along the main road and
in the hotels

🚌 Tourist shuttle buses to
most destinations in
Bali

♿ Few

↔ Museum Le Mayeur
(▶ 39)

*Sanur makes an excellent
base for water-sports
enthusiasts*

8
Ubud's Art Galleries

52B2

See Paintings, in Shopping (▶ 104)

Most galleries are open from 8–7 or even later

Restaurants ($–$$) within walking distance of galleries

Few

Galleries: free. Museum Neka: cheap

Ubud (▶ 50–5), Museum Neka (▶ 51), Puri Lukisan Museum (▶ 53), Penestanan (▶ 61)

There is an amazing display of indigenous artistic talent here, with paintings of all sizes in a variety of styles to suit all budgets.

Do you splash out on a huge canvas of bright green parrots in a tropical setting or opt instead for a detailed Batuan-style miniature where every inch of the canvas is intricately painted? There is more than one traditional style of pictorial painting, in addition to the expressionist work of the Young Artists school and the increasingly popular modernist style, which is often abstract in its subject matter. The choice is bewildering and a visit to Ubud's Museum Neka provides an educational introduction to the different styles and themes of Balinese painting; an advisable exercise before visiting some of the countless galleries dotted in and around Ubud. The Puri Lukisan Museum in Ubud, also displays works of art of a high standard. In a short time you will begin to recognize the different themes and styles and notice the qualitative differences between paintings with the same subject. Prices are not always a reliable guide because galleries differ in the percentage difference between their first asking price and the final price they are prepared to settle for; it may range from 15–60 per cent. The best approach is to shop around,

This painting by an Ubud artist, with its rich colours, is typical in its graphic portrayal of rural life

practise your bargaining skills, and trust your instincts when choosing a particular painting.

Some of the galleries recommended in this guide (▶ 104) are in central Ubud but quite a few are north of the town center, on either side of the main road in the vicinity of the Museum Neka. The village of Penestanan, less than an hour's walk from the center, is an especially delightful place to shop for paintings.

The larger galleries are able to arrange for a framed painting to be shipped home, but an alternative is to dispense with the frame and have the canvas wrapped in a sturdy, protective roll or tube.

9
Senggigi

This is the most developed and enjoyable beach-resort area in Lombok, and the best base for any visit to the island.

The range of restaurants and accommodation, and its laid-back atmosphere, help make Senggigi the ideal place for a relaxing holiday on Lombok. From the airport, which is in Mataram a few kilometers to the south, or the ferry port, at Lembar about 35km away, it takes little more than half an hour to reach the series of sweeping beaches at Senggigi and it is easy to arrange visits and tours to other parts of Lombok from here. A direct boat service goes to Gili Trawangan (*gili* means island in Sasak), and a Perama tourist bus office offers scheduled services to Bali (via ferry) as well as serving destinations around Lombok. Money changers, airline agents, car and bike hire operators, super-markets, tourist shops – all thinly spread across Lombok as a whole – are handily located along the one main road that defines Senggigi. The centre of Senggigi may be taken as the cluster of establishments across the road from the Lombok Intan Laguna hotel (▶ 103).

Five minutes to the north are shops (▶ 107) and the Sheraton hotel (▶ 103), while to the south are more shops and restaurants and the Pura Batu Bolong temple. The road north from Senggigi to Pemenang (22km) follows the coastline and has spectacular views.

Mornings and afternoons can be whiled away on the beach or in hotel swimming pools. Evenings are quiet affairs but there are enough decent restaurants to make dinner enjoyable. At sunset fishermen set out from Senggigi Beach in a long line, their lamps forming a beautiful display, and soothing sunsets can also be appreciated from nearby Pura Batu Bolong. There are several bars and discotheques.

One of the many deserted beaches near Senggigi

✚ 80A2

✉ 6km north of Ampenan

🍴 The widest range of restaurants ($–$$) on Lombok

🚌 Buses connect the ferry port (with onward connections to Bali), airport and other Lombok locations

♿ Few

↔ Gili Islands (▶ 21), Pura Batu Bolong (▶ 87), Sira (▶ 88)

25

10
Gunung Kawi

29E2

North of Tampaksiring, 15km north of Ubud

Daily 7–6

Restaurants ($) in Tampaksiring

Best visited with a tour

Cheap

Tirta Empul (➤ 64)

Off the main tourist trail, these 11th-century memorials are cut into the bare rock face at the bottom of a green valley.

There is no definitive explanation for these 7m-high memorial tombs (*candi*) but the likeliest explanation is that they were sculptured after the demise of an 11th-century king. Archaeologists tend to favor King Anak Wungsu of the Udayana dynasty, but no ashes or bones have been found here, so they are not burial tombs. Nothing is known of the builder artists, though legend credits the giant Kebo Iwa with the achievement of completing all the memorials in one long night using only his fingernails.

Legend maintains that a royal prince carved these shrines with his fingernails

As you first approach the river, four of the ten *candi* come into view. These are traditionally believed to be dedicated to the king's favourite concubines. The plastered exteriors have worn away, but it is possible to make out the shapes of the false doors that adorned each memorial. On the other side of the River Pakrisan there is a second cluster of five *candi* behind a set of rooms, believed to have been the cells of priests who looked after the site and conducted ceremonies. The five memorials may refer to King Udayana, Queen Mahendradata and their three sons. The tenth memorial is a ten-minute walk away to the south of the four *candi*, back on the other side of the river. It may be a dedication to an important minister or adviser to the royal family. The road to Gunung Kawi ('Mountain of the Poet') is signposted off to the right on the main road just to the north of Tampaksiring.

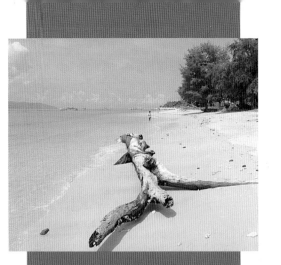

What To See

Above: *Gili Trawangan*

Right: *statue in Nusa Dua*

Laut Bali

Tanjung Batugondang
Pulau Menjangan
Gn. Prapat Agung 332m
Banyuwedang
Pulaki
Lovina Beach Resort ■
Ketapang
Kalibubuk
Labuhan Lalang
Penyabangan
Seririr
Gilimanuk
Jayaprana Grave Site
Cekik ■ Pura Bakungan
S. Sangian
Gn. Merbuk
1224m
Celukanbawang
Pengastulan
Brahma Arama Vihara, Hot Spring
Gn. Musi
1385m
Banjar Tega Hot Springs
Busungbiu
Gn. Mesehe 1344m
Taman Nasional Bali Barat (West Bali National Park)
S. Daya
S. Bilukpoleng
Yeh Sumbul
Pupuan
Melaya
Palahan
3
Negara
Mendoyo
Munduk
Pura Gede Prancak
Pura Rambut Siwi
Pulukan
Pekutatan
Yehbadian
Yehotix
Selat Bali
Tanjung Canding
Antosari
Bajera
2
Soka Antosari
Dukuh
Tanjung Keben
Black Sand Beach ■

Blambangan Nature Reserve
Jawa (Java)

0   10   20   30km

1

A   B   C

Many rural Balinese depend upon the farming of rice for their livelihoods

BALI

Tanjung Bungkulan
Kloncing angst
Kubutambahan
Alassari
Sanih
Jagaraga
Pura Dalem
Gedong Kertya
S. Daya
Tejakula
ukasada
Sawan
Sambirenteng
Gitgit
Pura Tegeh
Koripan
Tianyar
Salt Panning
Vehketipat
Danau
Buyan
1717m
Gn. Catur
Penulisan
Songan
1717m
Gn. Batur
Toya Bungkah
Terunyan
Danau
Tamblingan
Danau Bratan
Candikuning
Kintamani
Pura Batur
Danau
Batur
2153m
Gn. Abang
Tulamben
WWII Ship Wreck
Botanical
Gardens
Pura Ulun Danu
Bedugul
Penelokan
Kedisan
3142m
Gn. Agung
Amed
Bunutan
Baturiti
Pelaga
Pura Besakih
Culik
Tanjung
Ibus
Jatiluwih
Besakih
Abang
Kusambi
Seraya
ura Luhur
Batukau
Pura Yeh
Gangga
Tirta Empul
Pura
Sakenan
Rendang
Tirta Ayu
Tirtagangga
Pura
Lempuyang
Penebel
Tampaksiring
Gunung
Kawi
Selat
Iseh
Tenganan
Amlapura
Sangeh
Pura Kehen
Puri Taman Ujung
(Floating Palace)
Pura Bukit Sari
Pura Taman
Ayun
Ubud
Bangli
Candidasa
Tabanan
Goa Gajah
Gianyar
Klungkung
Tel. Amuk
Padangbai
rambitan
Kediri
Mengwi
Muncan
Mas
Blahbatuh
Kusamba
Goa Lawah (Bat Cave)
Selat Lombok
Sempidi
Yeh Ayung
Sukawati
Celuk
Batubulan
Selat Badung
Mabua Express to
Lembar (Lombok) 2–2.5hrs
Tanah
Lot
Ubung
Denpasar
Sanur
Beach
Resort
Nusa Lembongan
Jungutbatu
Pura Peed
Toyapakeh
Auto ferry to Lembar,
Lombok, 4 hr
Legian
Kuta
Nusa Ceningan
Nusa Penida
Pejukutan
Pura Batu Madan
Pura Batu Kuring
Ngurah Rai
International
Airport
Pulau Serangan
Benoa Harbour
Benoa
Tanjung
Benoa
Sebuluh
Waterfall
Jimbaran
Nusa Dua Beach Resort
Jluwatu
Nusa Dua
Tanjung
Mebulu
D
E
F

South &
Southeast Bali

The south of Bali is where all visitors to the island first arrive and is where a fair number spend all or most of their time. The airport is here, close to the administrative capital Denpasar and even closer to Kuta and other highly developed beach resort areas. Kuta is Bali's infamous tourist capital, enjoyed and abhorred in equal measure, while the nearby resort of Sanur offers a quieter alternative. Cultural highlights in the south include the ancient temples of Tanah Lot and Uluwatu, both perched on the shoreline like sentinels guarding the treasures that lay inland. The southeast of Bali is well worth exploring as an escape from the commercial hustle and bustle that is in danger of swamping parts of the south. A day or two spent in the small resort village of Candi Dasa is a perfect way to unwind.

'If anything, tourism has pumped more life into the Balinese cultural Renaissance that began earlier this century. There are probably more superb artists and craftsmen in Bali today than at any time in its history.'

International Herald Tribune
(1986)

Denpasar

Denpasar is probably one of the least-visited capitals of a major tourist destination, but this is partly because the hedonistic allure of Kuta is too strong to compete with and Denpasar has busied itself evolving into a working city in its own right. It has only been called Denpasar since 1949, when newly independent Bali asserted itself by shifting the capital from Singaraja in the north, where the Dutch had based themselves, to Badung in the south, which was then renamed Denpasar.

Denpasar translates as 'north of the market,' and the market itself is worth experiencing, even if you buy nothing. The more sedate Museum Bali (▶ 32), which is nearby, also merits a visit for an introduction to Balinese culture. The best way to enjoy Denpasar is by devoting a morning to walking around it (▶ 37) because this provides an opportunity to see a rare urban aspect to Bali. The city population is fast exceeding 400,000 and the Balinese share their city with an increasing number of Muslims from Java and Lombok, while Chinese immigrants run many of the shops and small businesses. There are plenty of non-tourist shops to browse through.

Public transport connects Denpasar with most corners of Bali but if you are based further south in Kuta, Sanur or Nusa Dua it may be worth traveling to and from Denpasar by taxi as many of the *bemo* stations are spread out around the city perimeter and away from the places of interest. There is little reason to stay overnight in Denpasar and the choice of restaurants is poor, so a morning visit is best (Museum Bali is not open in the afternoons).

Umbrellas, used by the Balinese for village events, on sale to tourists in Denpasar

What to See in Denpasar

MUSEUM BALI

This museum was founded by the Dutch in the early decades of this century but it wasn't completed until 1932. There are four sections to the museum, each housed in a separate building, and the main two-story building is the one facing the entrance. The ground floor has archaeological finds while upstairs contains farming equipment and sculptors' tools. The other three buildings contain an eclectic range of exhibits: ceremonial dress and accessories, religious artifacts, a model of a cremation ceremony, textiles, and spinning equipment. The building with the sandstone statues outside has splendid examples of both black and white magic characters from Balinese dances as well as some superb dance masks.

33A2
Jalan Letkol Wisnu, near Puputan Square in the centre of town
Sun–Thu 7–2, Fri 7–11, Sat 7–12:30. Closed: Mon
The nearest restaurant ($$) is at the Natour Bali Hotel in Jalan Veteran
Cheap

PASAR BADUNG

The grim exterior of the three-story building that houses the largest market in Denpasar gives little indication of the teeming life inside. The ground floor spills over with every type of fruit and vegetable grown on fertile Bali, and visitors are guaranteed to discover at least a dozen unknown examples of local food. The first floor is a warren of small shops dedicated to household goods and dried food, while the top floor is a pot-pourri of textiles, clothing and some handicrafts. Local women tend to persist in offering their services as guides, so a polite but firm refusal may be necessary.

33A2
Jalan Gajah Mada
Daily 7–6
Small cafés ($) in the adjoining streets
Tegal bemo station in Jalan Imam Bonjoi serves the southern peninsula, including Kuta and Sanur
Free

PURA JAGATNATA

Next door to the Museum Bali is the modern Pura Jagatnata temple, built in the 1950s though it looks older. All temples have a shrine-tower topped by an empty throne, known as the *padmasana*, and the one here is a particularly fine example made of white coral.

33A2
Jalan Letkol Wisnu
Daily 8–5
Cheap
A sash must be worn

TAMAN BUDAYA CULTURAL CENTRE

The main exhibition here focuses on the history of Balinese painting but this could be skipped if you are planning to visit Ubud's Museum Neka (► 51) which presents a more educational overview. Other exhibits are devoted to dance masks, woodcarving and other handicrafts. Traditional dances are performed most nights in the adjoining amphitheater and, in the summer months, there are often special exhibitions and performances.

33A2
Jalan Nusa Indah
Tue–Sun 8–5. Closed Mon
Small restaurant ($) in the center
Kereneng bemo station
Cheap

Museum Bali is a work of art in its own right

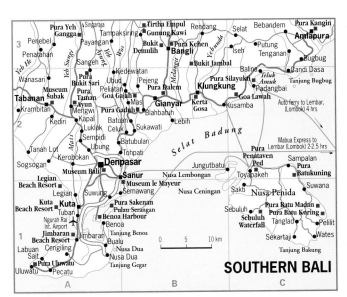

SOUTHERN BALI

Pura Yeh Gangga · Singaraja · Tirtha Empul · Rendang · Selat · Bebandem · Pura Kangin · Amlapura
Penebel · Payangan · Tampaksiring · Gunung Kawi · Bukit Demulih · Pura Kehen · Bangli · Iseh · Putung · Tenganan · Bugbug
Penatahan · Sangeh · Kedewatan · Bukit Jambal · Balina · Teluk Amuk · Candi Dasa · Tanjung Bugbug
Wanasari · Pura Bukit Sari · Ubud · Pejeng · Pura Dalem · Pura Silayuku · Padangbai
Museum Subak · Pura Taman Ayun · Peliatan · Goa Gajah · Mas · Pura Dalem · Klungkung · Kerta Gosa · Goa Lawah · Kusamba
Tabanan · Krambitan · Kediri · Mengwi · Kapal · Pura Gaduh · Blahbatuh · Gianyar · Lebih · Auto ferry to Lembar, (Lombok) 4 hrs
Lukluk · Batuan · Celuk · Sukawati · Selat Badung
Sempidi · Ubung · Batubulan · Tohpati · Mabua Express to Lembar (Lombok) 2-2.5 hrs
Kerobokan · Denpasar · Pura Penataven Ped · Sampalan · Pura Batukuning
Sogsogan · Museum Bali · Sanur · Jungutbatu · Toyapakeh · Suwana
Legian · Beach Resort · Museum le Mayeur · Nusa Lembongan · Sakti · Nusa Penida
Legian · Suwung · Semawang · Nusa Ceningan · Sebuluh · Pura Batu Madan
Kuta · Kuta · Pura Sakenan · Pura Batu Kuring · Tanglad · Pelilit
Beach Resort · Tuban · Pulau Serangan · Sebuluh Waterfall · Wates
Ngurah Rai Int. Airport · Benoa Harbour · Benoa
Jimbaran · Jimbaran · Tanjung Benoa · Bualu · Sekartaji
Beach Resort · Cengiling · Nusa Dua · Tanjung Bakung
Labuan Sait · Pura Uluwatu · Nusa Dua · Tanjung Gegar
Uluwatu · Pecatu

0 · 5 · 10 km

What to See in South & Southeast Bali

AMLAPURA ✪

This is the main town in southeast Bali and during the eruption of Gunung Agung in 1963 the town, then called Karangasem, was cut off by lava flow which flattened parts of the outskirts. The town was renamed so as to help remove any bad karma. The only attraction open for visitors is Puri Agung, one of the town's royal palaces, also known as Puri Kangin. The main structure inside this palace is the Maskerdam (a corruption of Amsterdam) building, named as a tribute to the Dutch who allowed the Karangasem royalty to retain more of their traditional privileges than granted to other Bali kingships. Unfortunately, the palace evokes little of its past splendors.

BATUBULAN ✪✪

This is a regular stop on the Denpasar to Ubud arts-and-crafts trail and the specialty here is stonecarving. The stone carvers work by the side of the road and it is fascinating to watch them chiseling away at huge blocks of stone. Small portable carvings of mythological figures are also on sale. The best place to appreciate examples of larger finished work is in the temple, Pura Puseh, reached by turning right when exiting from the north end of the village. Next to the temple is a dance stage where morning performances of the *Barong and Rangda* dance are held daily (► 112). Evening dances are also performed on a regular basis.

BENOA ✪✪

Benoa, also known as Tanjung Benoa, is a peninsula that points north from Nusa Dua. It has become a major watersports playground for the area and boats once used for fishing now ferry surfers and snorkelers. Other activities include parasailing, jetskiing and banana boat riding.

✚ 33C3
✉ Amlapura is 13km east of Candi Dasa. Puri Agung is on Jalan Gajah Mada
🕐 Puri Agung: daily 8–6
🚌 *Bemos*, which pass Puri Agung, serve Candi Dasa, Padangbai and Singaraja
✋ Puri Agung: cheap
↔ Tirtagangga (► 22), Candi Dasa (► 35), Tenganan (► 47), Amed (► 70), Wreck of the Liberty (► 76)

✚ 33A2
✉ 10km northeast of Denpasar
🚌 Batubulan *bemo* station is at the southern end of the village, with connections to Ubud and eastern Bali
✋ Pura Puseh: free
↔ Denpasar (► 31–2), Celuk (► 35)

✚ 33A1
✉ 5km north of Nusa Dua
🍴 A number of small restaurants ($) along the main road
🚌 *Bemos* shuttle between the northern tip of the Benoa peninsula and the Nusa Dua junction at the southern end
↔ Nusa Dua (► 39)

Ganesh, the elephant god, receives the finishing touches at Batubulan

34

CANDI DASA ✪✪✪

An increasing number of visitors are now spending a part of their time based in Candi (pronounced Chandy) Dasa, preferring it to the brashness of Kuta or the expense of Nusa Dua. Plenty of decent restaurants, a growing number of bars and shops, tourist amenities and a pleasant character to the resort (no pavement hawkers peddling fake watches and the like) make it an enjoyable accommodation center. It is well-situated for excursions further east and north and the Perama bus company has an office, on the main road in the center of town (☎ 0363-41114) for booking day trips.

A drawback for some is the absence of a beach (washed away when the reef was used as building material in the 1980s) but this helps to keep the crowds at bay and there is a sandy beach to the east which is within walking distance. Snorkeling and diving operators are easy to find.

✚ 33C2
✉ 69km northeast of Denpasar
🍴 Excellent range of restaurants ($–$$) either side of the resort's main road (▶ 92)
🚌 Bemos from Denpasar's Batubulan terminal stop at Candi Dasa en route to Amlapura
🔄 Amlapura (▶ 34), Padangbai (▶ 42), Tenganan (▶ 47)

Ornate stone statues, like this one at Candi Dasa, are a common sight in Bali

CELUK ✪✪

This is the second stop on the Denpasar to Ubud arts-and-crafts trail. Here the specialty is silverwork: earrings, necklaces, chains, rings, bracelets and brooches. The village is basically a 3km-strip of main road defined by small and large jewelry shops (▶ 105) on both sides. This is a village dedicated to shopping – there are no places to stay and no restaurants. As a general rule, it pays to avoid the grander-looking jewelry shops that provide large parking spaces for tour coaches and seek out instead the smaller establishments.

✚ 33B2
✉ 12km northeast of Denpasar
🚌 Bemos running between Denpasar's Batubulan terminal and Ubud stop in Celuk
🔄 Batubulan (▶ 34), Batuan (▶ 57)

GIANYAR ✪

A busy town with an illustrious history but of minimal interest to tourists. There is a variety of temples and a few craft villages dotted around to the west and south but the pretty coastline near the temples is not safe for swimming. Furthermore, despite being famous for *babi guling* (roast pig) there is no tourist-oriented restaurant in the town.

✚ 33B2
✉ 10km southeast of Ubud
🚌 Bemos from Denpasar

GOA LAWAH

Goa Lawah, very popular with tours, is a bat cave in a cliff which is also home to a small highly revered temple. Countless thousands of fruit bats inhabit the cave and they will probably be heard and smelled before being seen. Legend tells of a giant snake deep inside the cave which is fed by the bats. An unfortunate aspect of Goa Lawah is the temerity and tenacity of the hawkers, who will press free gifts on visitors as their opening gambit.

🗺 33C2
✉ 9km east of Klungkung
🕐 Daily 7–6
🚌 *Bemos* from Denpasar's Batubulan terminal stop en route to Amlapura
✋ Cheap
↔ Klungkung (▶ 36), Padangbai (▶ 42)

JIMBARAN ✪✪✪

This fishing village is south of the airport and boasts an excellent crescent-shaped beach that is never crowded. Jimbaran boasts dozens of open-air, beachside seafood restaurants. Sunset is the best time to visit for views and to ensure the pick of the catch, which includes prawns, squid, lobster and snapper, all grilled before your eyes.

🗺 33A1
✉ 2km south of the airport
🍴 Excellent restaurants ($$–$$$) in the hotels
♿ Few
↔ Uluwatu (▶ 16), Kuta (▶ 38), Nusa Dua (▶ 39)

KAPAL

This little village is noteworthy for its sculptors and its temple but they are only worth seeing if passing through on a journey (▶ 45). Shops displaying their wares of sculptured figures line both sides of the main road. The temple of Pura Sadat dates back to the 12th century, though the present structure was mostly built in 1949 after the original was destroyed in an earthquake.

🗺 33A2
✉ 12km northwest of Denpasar
↔ Pura Taman Ayun (▶ 44), Tanah Lot (▶ 47)

KLUNGKUNG ✪✪✪

The royal palace in the town of Klungkung was home to Bali's most important dynasty until Dutch usurpation in 1908. What remains, inside a landscaped area known as Taman Gili, is the Kerta Gosa (Hall of Justice) – a legal chamber where participants could gaze at ceiling paintings of wrongdoers being punished by devils and the virtuous enjoying heavenly bliss. The famous paintings that can be gazed at today were completed in the 1940s. Also to be seen is the Bale Kambang (Floating Pavilion), said to be used for royal tooth-filing ceremonies. There is also a small museum which relates the history of Klungkung.

🗺 33B2
✉ 40km east of Denpasar
🕐 Royal Palace: daily 8–6
🚌 *Bemos* from Denpasar to Candi Dasa and Amlapura stop in Klungkung. *Bemos* also run to and from Besakih
✋ Royal palace and Bale Kambang: cheap. Museum: cheap

The Kerta Gosa at Klungkung ceased to function after the town fell to the Dutch in 1908

A Walk in Denpasar

This walk begins outside the Bali Natour Hotel.

With the main entrance to the hotel behind you, turn right and walk 100m to the roundabout where Jalan Gajah Mada meets Jalan Surapati. Turn left onto Jalan Surapati until the imposing residence of the governor of Bali is reached, then cross the road to reach the monument and fountain in the park of Puputan Square.

You are following in the footsteps of the last *raja* of Badung and more than a thousand of his people who in 1906 left their palace (now the governor's residence) and committed ritual suicide (called *puputan*, meaning 'ending') in the square rather than surrender to the overwhelming Dutch forces.

Walk to the left (eastern) side of the square.

Here Pura Jagatnata (▶ 32) and the Museum Bali (▶ 32) can be visited.

With the museum on your left, walk down to the first junction and turn right, with the south side of the square on your right. Walk straight across the next two junctions onto Jalan Kalimantan.

When walking on Jalan Kalimantan you will pass a good *warung* (a small street-side restaurant ▶ 97) and a traditional perfume shop.

Turn right when you reach a T-junction.

This street, Jalan Sulawesi, has small textile shops.

Cross to the other side of this street before the next crossroads.

Here is the main entrance to the Pasar Badung market (▶ 32). From the market it is a short walk north to the main road, Jalan Gajah Mada.

Turn right onto this busy commercial street.

Jalan Gajah Mada leads to the roundabout close to the Bali Natour Hotel where the walk began.

Distance
3km

Time
2–5 hours, depending on temple, museum and market visits

Start/end point
Bali Natour Hotel, near Puputan Square
➕ 33A2
🚌 Tegal *bemo* terminal

Lunch
Puri Agung restaurant ($$) (▶ 92) in the Bali Natour Hotel
✉ Jalan Veteran
☎ 0361-225681

A monument in Puputan Square pays homage to the heroic victims of resistance to the Dutch in 1906

KUTA

✪✪✪

Kuta is an extraordinary place and no one could have foreseen its development from a 17th-century slave port to an international beach resort pulsating slavishly to the tourist rhythm. A trickle of visitors began in the late 1930s but it wasn't until the 1960s that this started to become a gradual flood. Now, after some 40 years of dedicating itself to tourism, Kuta must have reached its zenith. The thousands of souvenir shops, pubs, restaurants, hotels, boutiques, money-changers and the like have filled every available foot of ground and it is difficult to imagine any further developments.

The neighboring areas of Tuban, Legian and Seminyak have merged with Kuta to form an 8km stretch, which soon makes walking tiresome. Use the metered taxis when necessary. The main road is Jalan Legian with narrow lanes and smaller streets joining it to the beachside road that runs parallel. In this area, between these roads, lies the heart of Kuta; a few bars in particular attract rowdy groups of young Australians. There are plenty of other pleasant bars and restaurants to enjoy between shopping trips (➤ 105,106,108,109), and Kuta's beach is superb for swimming, surfing or simply sunbathing.

Did you know ?

In 1936 an American couple, Bob and Louise Koke, came from California to Kuta and, impressed by the tourist potential of the beautiful beach, decided to build a small hotel which flourished until 1942 when non-paying Japanese guests turned up uninvited. The site of Bali's first hotel is now home to the Natour Kuta Beach Hotel (➤ 101).

MUSEUM LE MAYEUR   ◑◑

Adrien Le Mayeur (1880–1958) was a Belgian artist who settled in southern Bali in the 1930s, when he was in his early fifties, and married Ni Polok, a locally famous and stunningly beautiful *legong* dancer who was a teenager at the time. Their new home was built on the beach in Sanur and after Ni Polok's death in 1985 the house became a museum. The paintings on display are not as interesting as the building itself, which has been little altered over the years and retains its original carved windows and doors. The museum is at the northern end of Sanur's beachfront (turn right at the bottom of Jalan Hang Tuah).

- 🔲 33A2
- ✉ On Sanur's beachfront
- 🕐 Tue–Thu 8–2, Fri 8–1:30, Sun 8–4. Closed: Sat
- 🍴 Restaurants ($–$$) within walking distance
- 🚌 Denpasar *bemos* stop nearby on Jalan Hang Tuah
- 💷 Cheap
- ↔ Sanur (► 23)

NUSA DUA   ◑◑

This is a purpose-built upmarket beach resort, on the eastern tip of the Bukit peninsula, made up of internationally famous five-star hotels (► 101) rubbing shoulders with one another and nearly all running down to the beach. Nusa Dua is Bali's showcase resort, with its biggest convention centers complementing the exclusive hotels.

- 🔲 33A1
- ✉ 25km south of Denpasar
- 🍴 Many of the best restaurants in Bali ($$$)
- ♿ Few
- ↔ Uluwatu (► 16), Jimbaran (► 36)

There is a good beach, though bathers tend to prefer their hotel swimming pools. Guest facilities are second to none and it would be easy to stay here a week or more and never visit the same restaurant or bar a second time. Unfortunately, the only distraction to hotel life is the centrally located Galleria complex (► 109) which consists of top-end consumer outlets selling clothes and brand-name goods, and restaurants which are almost as expensive, but not as good as the ones in the hotels. If you are without your own transport you will have to rely on taxis, the free buses to the Galleria or the hotel shuttle-bus trips to Kuta.

Alone with the surf on the famous Kuta beach

39

Food & Drink

Meals in Bali are international in their variety and, with the exception of five-star hotels, inexpensive. Western favorites like pizza and pasta are ubiquitous, and the fast-food franchises have reached Kuta, but it is the fish and Indonesian dishes that will deliver novel and interesting tastes.

Indonesian Cuisine

The seafood can be relied on for its freshness and variety

A typical Indonesian meal will be based around rice, with side dishes of fish, vegetables and meat, and with the flavor mostly provided by chillis, ginger, turmeric and soy sauce. Fresh, local seafood is definitely worth enjoying

more than once. Starters and desserts are not common in Indonesian cuisine and versions of Western favorites may disappoint. Balinese dishes can be difficult to find but many of the smarter restaurants now feature some on their menu. *Babi guling* (roast suckling pig) is a favorite at festivals but not easily served up in a restaurant at short notice. Common dishes are *nasi goreng* (vegetables and some meat and/or fish with fried rice) and *nasi campur* (with boiled rice).

Drinking Water
Do not drink tap water and use bottled mineral water even for brushing your teeth. The ice served with drinks in most tourist restaurants should be reliable but there is no way to be sure; take care in smaller establishments, especially in Lombok.

Vegetarian Food

Vegetarians will have no problem finding non-meat dishes. *Gado-gado* (steamed bean sprouts and fresh vegetables laced together with a spicy peanut sauce) is found on every menu and *cap cai* (pronounced chap chy), which is basically stir-fried vegetables, is also very common. It is easy to tire of these, though, so look out for tofu-based dishes (pronounced tahu) which are often imaginatively prepared. The few vegetarian restaurants in Kuta and Ubud are well worth seeking out.

Durians

For a food experience that is truly different, try the infamous durian. The custard and almond taste is sheer heaven to durian devotees but most people are repulsed by the extremely pungent smell. Alfred Russel Wallace claimed they were 'worth a voyage to the East to experience'. Most definitely an acquired taste.

Other Tropical Fruits

The tropical fruits available in Bali are delicious and should not be missed when they are in season. The papaya, guava and mango may all be familiar enough, so try the rambutan, with red spiky hairs on the outside and a white and juicy fruit inside. Star fruit is readily identified by its shape, and the yellower the fruit the sweeter and riper the taste. Mangosteen's purple-brown shell hides a white fleshy fruit inside, while the *salak*, known also as the snake fruit, is the strangest-looking of all; peel its scaly brown shell to get at the luscious, segmented fruit inside. The heavyweight of all the tropical fruits is the jackfruit, weighing up to 20kg, with a knobbly green skin and a yellow segmented fruit inside.

Durian (top), rambutan (left), durian, bananas, and papaya (above)

Something to Drink?

Bottled soft drinks, coffee (*kopi*) and tea (*teh*) are widely available, though the local coffee is served black and unfiltered. Opinion varies as to the taste quality of local beers (*Bali Hai, Bintang, Anker*) but imported beers are becoming more common and tourist bars will stock imported spirits. The strongest local spirit is *arak* (distilled from rice), best mixed with 7-Up, or try *brem* (a rice wine) or *tuak* (a beer brewed from the sap of palm trees).

NUSA LEMBONGAN

This small island, 4km by 3km, has seen much development in recent years, but still retains a lot of its secluded charm. Reached on a variety of day trips, it is a popular water-sports destination. At low tide it is possible to wade across to Nusa Ceningan, an uninhabited tiny island off the south coast. Basic accommodation and food is available in the village of Jungutbatu on the west coast. There is not enough water to sustain rice growing and the cultivation of seaweed is the main livelihood of the 2,000 inhabitants. Bamboo frames in the water are used to train the seaweed which is then dried and sold as ingredients for cosmetics and food.

NUSA PENIDA

This island, close to Nusa Lembongan, has the interesting temple of Pura Pentaram Ped, a large limestone cave and a beautiful stretch of beach along the north coast. Sampalan is the largest town but the place to head for is Toyapakeh, in the northeast of the island, close to the lovely white beach. The south coast has spectacular scenery but a hired motorcycle is necessary to get there and the roads are not well maintained. The Balinese believe Nusa Penida is home to Jero Gede Macaling, a demon whose evil influence needs to be placated through ceremony and prayer.

PADANGBAI

Padangbai, the port for ferry boats to Lombok and tourist trips to Nusa Penida has responded to the tourist trade by developing accommodation and restaurants and is a very pleasant place to stay for a night or two. Snorkeling gear may be hired and there are three temples perched on the eastern headland of the crescent-shaped bay. The most significant of these is Pura Silayukti, reputedly the abode of an important priest in the 11th century.

+ 33B2

✉ 20km off the southeast coast

🍴 Restaurants ($) in Jungutbatu

📷 Catch a boat from Sanur (ticket office at the northern end of Sanur beach, in front of the Ananda Hotel, near the Museum Le Mayeur). Bali Hai Cruises (☎ 0361 720331)

↔ Nusa Penida (► below)

? It is usually necessary to stay overnight as boats depart for Sanur each morning. Package trips are available from the ticket office (see above)

Idyllic bungalows for an overnight stay on Nusa Lembongan

+ 33C1

✉ 22km off the southeast coast

🍴 Simple food available in Sampalan ($)

📷 Boats from Padangbai (► below)

↔ Nusa Lembongan (► above), Pura Penataran Ped (► 44)

+ 33C2

✉ 56km northeast of Denpasar

🍴 Small beach-front seafood restaurants ($)

🚌 Buses to Denpasar and most other destinations

↔ Nusa Lembongan and Nusa Penida (► above)

PANTAI SULUBAN ✪

Pantai means beach and Suluban Beach is a famous surfing spot visited religiously by keen surfers drawn by the powerful swell of the breaks. Non-surfers come here to enjoy the atmosphere and relax in the small bars and restaurants that have developed into a mini resort of their own. The beach, which unfortunately is not suitable for swimming, is at the end of a 3km-long track and boys with motorbikes are on hand to taxi people there.

🔲 33A1
✉ 22km south of Kuta
🍴 Small restaurants ($) facing the surf
🔄 Uluwatu (▶ 16)

PULAU SERANGAN ✪

This little island is also known as Turtle Island because of the practice of keeping turtles here until they weigh enough to slaughter and sell. The island is 3km long and less than half a kilometre wide and, apart from the Pura Sakenan temple which dates from the 16th century, there is little to see. Notwithstanding the relaxed atmosphere that characterizes the island – there are no roads or traffic – a snorkeling trip is the best reason for making a visit to Pulau Serangan.

🔲 33A1
✉ 400m south of Sanur
🍴 Small places serving local seafood ($)
🚤 The easiest way to get here is on a snorkeling trip, readily bookable in Sanur, Nusa Dua or Kuta

PURA DALEM ✪✪

Pura dalem means 'temple of the dead' and every village has one but the *pura dalem* near Gianyar is one of the better examples. It is dedicated to the witch Rangda, who can be seen performing vile deeds in the sculptures near the gate. The tower with the drum bell (the *kulkul* tower), used to summon devotees, is decorated with further unpleasant images of the fate awaiting those sent to hell. There is also a small shrine in front of the temple built in honour of Merajapati, the caretaker of the dead.

🔲 33B2
✉ 3km from Gianyar on the road to Bangli
🕐 Daily 8–4
🎫 Free
🔄 Bangli (▶ 56)
❓ A sash must be worn

Above: *The beach at Padangbai, with Nusa Penida in the background*

PURA LUHUR ULUWATU (▶ 16, TOP TEN)

43

PURA PENATARAN PED ✪

➕ 33C2
✉ 5km east of Toyapakeh on Nusa Penida
🕐 Daily 8–6
💲 Cheap
↔ Nusa Lembongan (➤ 42), Nusa Penida (➤ 42)
❓ A sash must be worn

This temple of the dead is on Nusa Penida and is dedicated to Jero Gede Macaling (➤ 42). Its conventional three courtyards are larger than normal because this is an important temple for the Balinese and its anniversary festival attracts a large gathering. The inner courtyard is the most interesting because of its large shrine with skillfully carved doors.

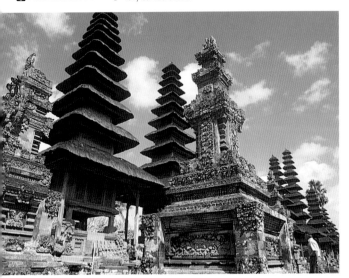

The meru *is one of the most characteristic features of Balinese temple architecture*

PURA TAMAN AYUN ✪✪

➕ 33A2
✉ Mengwi village, 18km northwest of Denpasar
🕐 Daily 8–6
🍴 Many small restaurants ($) close to the temple
🚌 *Bemos* from Denpasar to Bedugul stop at Mengwi
💲 Cheap
↔ Tanah Lᴏᵗ (➤ 47), Sangeh Monkey Forest (➤ 63)
❓ A sash must be worn. Outside the temple is a small museum

This large temple, dating back to 1634 and renovated in the 1930s, was the chief place of worship for the Mengwi kingdom until the end of the 19th century. It is now a regular stop on many coach tours. It has an unusually large number of the small multi-tiered shrines (*meru*) that are found in all temples and the inner courtyard has a small moat. The outside of the temple is picturesquely surrounded by another, broader moat filled with lotus flowers and lilies. It is thought the palace was designed to model Mount Meru, the mythical home of the Balinese gods surrounded by sea.

SANUR (➤ 23, TOP TEN)

South Bali Drive

This drive begins in Kuta, on the main road heading north out of town through Legian and Seminyak. Early in the morning all the traffic will be heading for work in the opposite direction. Other Balinese will already be at work: women on building sites carrying up to 15 bricks on their heads, villagers selling watermelons by the side of the road, farmers tending rice paddies.

Follow the signs for Sempidi and Tabanan.

You will pass through Kapal (➤ 36) with its roadside shops.

A junction is soon reached where the signs point north for Mengwi and west for Tanah Lot and Gilimanuk.

A diversion could be taken to Mengwi to visit Pura Taman Ayun (➤ 44) but, if so, return to this junction.

At this junction follow the sign for Tanah Lot. Along this road, approximately 18km from Kuta, a T-junction is reached. A sign points left for Tanah Lot, 10km to the south.

The temple at Tanah Lot (➤ 47) is on a rocky outcrop out at sea.

Return 10km to the main road where, instead of turning right for Denpasar, carry straight on (passing a bemo station on the right).

It is 1.5km from the *bemo* station to the Subak Museum (➤ 46). Look for a red sign on the left at the bottom of a hill for the Taliwang Bersaudara restaurant. (If you find yourself on a dual carriageway, with a model policeman on duty in the center of the road, you have gone too far.) This restaurant is next to the museum.

From Tabanan retrace the route to Kuta.

Distance
40km (including Tanah Lot)

Time
5 hours

Start/end point
Kuta
🕂 33A1

Lunch
Taliwang Bersaudara
restaurant ($)
✉ Tabanan

Did you know ?

*A temple (*pura*) is conceived as a home for the gods when they are not in heaven and is best visited during its anniversary celebrations (*odalan*) when villagers pull out all the stops in making their temple as dramatic and attractive as possible. The* odalan *is an open invitation to the gods to pay a visit so that they can be showered with gifts and displays of gratitude. The statues are covered with coloured cloth and women make their ceremonial entrance carrying stupendous pyramids of fruit and flowers on their heads, but still maintaining incredible poise and balance. Temple etiquette demands that all visitors show respect to the gods by wearing a ceremonial sash. These can usually be hired at the temple or purchased from any fabric shop. A sarong may be required at some temples and skimpy clothing is generally discouraged.*

45

SUBAK MUSEUM ⭐⭐

This museum is not on the tourist trail (and is easy to miss, ➤ 45 for road directions) but is well worth a visit for those with an interest in agriculture. Interesting exhibits include an *okdkan* (a wooden box used for farming festivals), the three types of rice plough, and fish-catching implements for use in the rice fields. Visitors are so few that the place may well be opened up just for you and the caretaker is happy to explain and describe the exhibits. The Taliwang Bersaudara restaurant is next to the museum.

SUKAWATI ⭐⭐

This is another stop on the arts-and-crafts trail between Denpasar and Ubud, and the chief attraction is its centrally located craft market. There is a wide choice of fabrics and this is the place to buy a ceremonial sash for temple visits. Also on sale are sarongs, cloth by the meter, light blankets that serve as bedspreads, and a multitude of baskets, wind chimes and temple umbrellas.

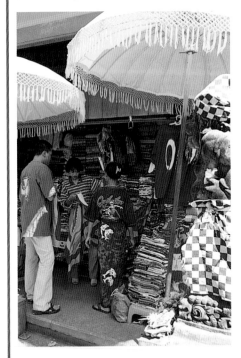

From sunrise to sunset the shops of Sukawati beckon

TABANAN ✪

Tabanan is one of the eight districts of Bali, and is the name of Tabanan district's capital town. There is little of interest in the town itself, apart from the Subak Museum, but with your own transport it is possible to explore the small villages and coastline to the south. If you head west from Tabanan for 3km, on the main road to Negara, you can take the left turning for Krambitan. This little village is home to royal palaces, both of which may be visited. The road continues south to the coast at Dukuh, where there is a lovely black-sand beach and safe swimming.

🞢 33A2
✉ 18km northeast of Denpasar
🍴 Taliwang Bersaurada restaurant ($), next to the Subak Museum
🚌 *Bemos* between Denpasar and Gilimanuk stop in Tabanan
🔁 Pura Taman Ayun (▶ 44), Subak Museum (▶ 46), Tanah Lot (▶ 47)

TANAH LOT ✪✪✪

This temple's location, perched on a rock with waves crashing about it, is beautiful and viewing the multi-tiered shrines against the falling light of approaching sunset is indeed a memorable event. Unfortunately, this is known to every tour operator in Bali so you will not be alone. With your own transport it is worth turning up for sunrise, when the dawn colors also lend dramatic splendor to the distinctive silhouette of the temple. When the tide is out it is possible to clamber over the rocks to the temple base. A 16th-century Javanese monk, Nirartha, is credited with founding the temple, which is regarded as an especially holy place. Nirartha went on to establish the Uluwatu temple (▶ 16).

🞢 33A2
✉ 30km northwest of Denpasar
🕐 Ticket office: 7–6:30; viewing possible any time
🍴 Several places to eat ($–$$) in the vicinity
🚌 *Bemos* from Denpasar to Gilimanuk pass through Kediri; then to Tanah Lot
💰 Cheap
🔁 Subak Museum (▶ 46), Tabanan (▶ 47)

TENGANAN ✪✪

Tenganan is a Bali Aga village, inhabited by descendants of the original Balinese who predate the arrival of the Javanese Majapahit kingdom in the 14th century. The village, easily visited from nearby Candi Dasa, has 150 families making up a population of 370. Upon reaching the village you will be met by an English-speaking villager who will act as a guide. Not surprisingly, the tour includes opportunities to purchase village-produced items like bamboo calendars, baskets and batik. A special type of cloth (*geringsing*) is woven in the village but it is expensive. During the summer months a number of festivals are held here and the event to try and catch is the *Perang Padan* (held between mid-June and early July) when mock but bloody fights are held using the thorny leaves of the pandanus as weapons.

To get to Tenganan follow the road signposted to the village, just to the west of Candi Dasa. After about 1.5km turn left for another 1.5km. Bicycles may be hired in Candi Dasa.

🞢 33C3
✉ 4km north of Candi Dasa
💰 Cheap (you will be asked to sign the visitors' book and make a donation)
🔁 Candi Dasa (▶ 35)

Central & West Bali

This section covers the town of Ubud, the most popular destination outside of southern Bali, as well as some of the least-visited parts of the island. Such is the growing popularity of the Ubud area that an increasing number of visitors choose to base themselves inland in Ubud rather than at the established beach resorts to the south. The arts-and-crafts villages around Ubud offer a pastoral idyll and a rewarding chance for visitors to experience the 'real Bali', a unique balance of beautiful countryside, friendly people, and a fascinating culture that seems to happily absorb tourism rather than be weakened by it.

The western side of Bali, by comparison, is rarely visited because, although there is some spectacular scenery, the population density is low and the tourist infrastructure is thin on the ground.

> *' In Ubud (heart of Bali heart of the world) the arts have thrived forever and the roots of a foreign community have been feeling their way into this outlandish soil. '*
>
> INEZ BARANAY
> *The Saddest Pleasure* (1989)

———————•———————

Facing page: *Puri Saren Agung detail*

Ubud

Ubud has the unrivaled claim to be the cultural heart and soul of Bali. The masses of small shops, dedicated to paintings, woodwork and other arts and crafts, give the town a real market feel, but beware that much of the 'art' is now mass-produced. Ubud is best seen on foot, with both the town and surrounding rural countryside highly amenable to meandering walks. The cooler, if slightly damper, climate provides permanently fresh, unpolluted air, making it a favorite town for so many visitors to Bali.

Ever since the artist Walter Spies came to Ubud in the late 1920s travelers have been following in his footsteps, yet, despite the tremendous increase in numbers, the town retains its charm and rarely disappoints those who stay. The atmosphere is subdued and easygoing and it is not a difficult place in which to relax. Quite apart from the absorbing enjoyment of cultural shopping, Ubud offers the best-value dining opportunities anywhere in Bali. Restaurateurs have responded to the tourist market with the same talent and flair that characterizes the work of local artists. The quality of accommodation, in Ubud and in the neighboring villages, is equally impressive and caters to all budgets.

Framed and ready to go at one of Ubud's many art galleries

The original village of Ubud has now grown into a town that includes once-neighboring villages like Penestanan and Peliatan, but the central crossroads remains the junction where Ubud Palace meets Monkey Forest Road (the tourist information office is here also). The surrounding countryside is easily reached by a short walk or cycle to the west where, uniquely, one may wander through hamlets where the wonders of nature and agriculture compete for your attention with local artists' displays of paintings and other arts.

What to See in Ubud

ANTONIO BLANCO'S HOUSE ✪

Opinions differ as to the worth of a visit to the theatrical home-turned-gallery of the most flamboyant of Ubud's contemporary expatriate artists. His paintings, mostly exotic ones of semi-clad females, adorn the walls and there is no mistaking the artist's personality, which impresses itself upon every room.

✚ 52B2
✉ Off Jalan Raya Campuan
🕐 Daily 7–5
🍴 Restaurants ($–$$) within walking distance
✋ Cheap

MONKEY FOREST ✪✪

The monkeys here are too used to tourists and they can aggressively pester anyone who they think is hiding food. Keep a tight hold on any valuables, as the monkeys are known to grab more than just food. More interesting and less demanding is the *pura dalem* (temple of the dead) situated inside the forest. There are restaurants on Monkey Forest road.

✚ 52B2
✉ At the south end of Monkey Forest Road
🕐 Daily 7–6
🍴 Restaurants ($–$$)
✋ Cheap
↔ Nyuhkuning (▶ 60)

MUSEUM NEKA ✪✪

This is the one of the best galleries in Bali and should not be missed. The first of the rooms displays examples of the major schools of Balinese art, the earliest being the traditional two-dimensional Kamasan style which gave way in the 1930s to the Ubud style, influenced by Western artists with their notions of perspective and much concerned with the effects of light and shadow. The Batuan style is best represented by *Busy Bali* by Wayan Bendi, packed with dense details (including tourists all with long noses!). A second room is devoted to Bali's best known artist Gusti Nyoman Lempad (▶ 52); his paintings of tales from Indian epics and local folklore are very well explained in the museum, and his *Mother & Father Brayut* series and his *Battle at Langkapura* are deservedly popular. Another room, displaying works from other parts of Indonesia, has the astonishing *Three Masked Dancers* by Anton Kustia Widjaja. The final room, entitled 'East meets West', has the work of foreign artists upstairs and paintings by the famous Javanese artist Affandi downstairs. A bookstore at the museum sells books on Balinese art and culture.

✚ 52B2
✉ Jalan Raya Campuan
☎ 0361-975074
🕐 Daily 9–5
🍴 Café ($) in grounds

Above: *painting in the Museum Neka*

🚌 *Bemos* heading west stop outside the museum; hail *bemos* outside to return to the center of Ubud
✋ Cheap
↔ Penestanan (▶ 61)

NYOMAN LEMPAD'S HOUSE

Bali's best-known artist, Gusti Nyoman Lempad, was born in the village of Gianyar but later moved to Ubud where he lived until his death, in 1978, at the apparent age of 116. He is most famous for his ink drawings on paper and while the Museum Neka (▶51) has first-class examples of his talent there is very little on display at his home, which is now open to the public.

PURA CAMPUAN

This temple, also known as Pura Gunung Lebah, stands at the confluence of two rivers and may be visited as part of an enjoyable walk in the Ubud countryside (▶54). The temple was renovated in 1991 and contains more than a dozen small, thatched shrines and a large, colored statue of a dancing god. To reach the temple from Antonio Blanco's house (▶51), cross the road and take the first turning on the left on the other side of the bridge, on the road back into the center of Ubud. Soon after turning left, turn left again down the steps at the sign that reads 'Going to the Hill'.

✝ 52B2
✉ Off Jalan Raya
🕐 Daily 8–5
🍴 Restaurants nearby ($) on Jalan Raya
✋ Free

✝ 52B2
✉ Campuan, less than 1km west of town center
🕐 24 hours daily
🍴 Restaurants nearby on the main road
✋ Free
↔ Penestanan (▶61)

Right: *Small thatched shrines at Pura Campuan*

PURA SARASWATI ✪✪

This little temple is famous for its fine examples of Gusti Nyoman Lempad's work (▶ 52). He designed the temple layout and executed the stone carvings that are so attractive a feature of this temple. Especially noteworthy is the rococo lotus-throne shrine upon which photographers practise their close-up techniques. It is upheld as one of Ubud's great examples of artistry. The name of the temple, Saraswati, refers to a revered Hindu river and its associated goddess.

PURI LUKISAN MUSEUM ✪✪

Puri Lukisan, Palace of Fine Arts, following extensive renovation in recent years, now forms a useful complement to the Museum Neka. It was founded in the mid-1950s through the combined efforts of an Ubud prince and the Dutch artist Rudolf Bonnet (1895–1978). These two men had been earlier closely involved in the *Pita Maha* movement, which developed as a response to the first wave of tourist interest in Bali. The movement sought to preserve artists' integrity while also integrating it with more Western influences, and the success of this venture may be judged by the high standard of much of the work on display in the Puri Lukisan. The gallery is set in lovely grounds with ponds, fountains and gorgeous flowers.

UBUD'S ART GALLERIES (▶ 24, TOP TEN)

🚩 52B2
✉ Off Jalan Raya, shortly before the Puri Lukistan Museum
🕐 24 hours daily
🍴 Restaurants ($) within walking distance on Jalan Raya
🎟 Free

🚩 52B2
✉ Jalan Raya
🕐 Daily 8–5
🍴 Restaurants ($–$$) within walking distance on Jalan Raya
🎟 Cheap
🔄 Penestanan (▶ 61)

A detail from the serene gardens surrounding Puri Lukisan Museum in Ubud

A Walk in the Ubud Countryside

Distance
12km (6km if a *bemo* is used to return to Ubud)

Time
4 hours (2 hours if a *bemo* is used to return to Ubud)

Start point
Pura Campuan
🔲 52B2

End point
Lungsiakan village (with the option of continuing to Penestanan)
🔲 52B2
🚌 Any *bemo* traveling towards Ubud

Lunch
Bridge Café ($$ (► 58). The Bridge Café is 1km after the Hotel Tjampuhan on the main road towards Ubud
✉ Campuan
☎ 0361-975085

This walk begins at Pura Campuan (► 52).

Behind Pura Campuan walk up the paved path.

You will see thatched hotel bungalows on your right and fields of elephant grass on both sides. Farmers are likely to be seen cutting the grass into bundled stoops for thatching or bringing their ducks to the rice paddies. The path gradually levels out and the main road can be glimpsed to the left.

Shortly after the paved path ends, the small Wayan Wijaya painting gallery (► 104) is passed and a path leads to a village. At the end of this village a café sells ice cream. Carry straight along the path to a larger village, at the end of which a junction is reached.

You should now be at the Lumbung Sari gallery.

Instead of carrying straight on (which would lead to Keliki) turn left and follow the path which crosses a bridge.

You will pass through the villages of Payogan and Lungsiakan.

The path comes out on the main road and the center of Ubud is 6km away to the left. Any bemo *traveling in this direction may be hailed or, if still feeling fit, walk 2km in the direction of Ubud as far as the Hotel Tjampuhan (► 102), cross the road and take the small road.*

This leads to the delightful village of Penestanan (► 61).

'Behind Pura Campuan walk up the paved path...'

PURI SAREN AGUNG

More commonly known as Ubud Palace, this building stands at the T-junction formed by Jalan Raya and Monkey Forest Road. Until the 1940s it was home to the local ruling dynasty. The compound is now open to the public who may wander around at will. It is best visited twice: once in daylight, when artistic details can be picked out on the sculptures and woodwork, and then again at night when the interior is dramatically lit for the regular dance performances.

52B2
Jalan Raya, north end of Monkey Forest Road
24 hours daily
Ubud's restaurants ($–$$) are all around
Free

Bougainvillea at Puri Saren Agung

SENIWATI GALLERY OF ART BY WOMEN

This gallery was established by Mary Northmore, a British expatriate artist, and is dedicated to redressing the male bias that features in most galleries of Balinese art. Some of the work on display is for sale and the gallery has a small shop around the corner on Jalan Raya selling other arts and crafts produced by women.

52B2
Jalan Sriwedari
0361-975485
Daily 9–5
Restaurants ($) on Jalan Raya
Free

WALTER SPIES' HOME

The German artist Walter Spies (1895–1942) settled in Ubud in the late 1920s and built a split-level bungalow-style home outside the village in Campuhan, overlooking the Wos Barat river. He designed the swimming pool (still in use) and entertained famous guests like Charlie Chaplin, before turning his home into a guest house which later expanded to become the Hotel Tjampuhan (▶ 102). Hotel staff are happy to point out Spies' home, presently the hotel's largest room but one which may eventually be developed into a memorial museum. It is worth wandering through the hotel's beautifully landscaped, riverside grounds. Spies is remembered as the choreographer of the spectacular 'monkey' dance now called the kecak.

52B2
Hotel Tjampuhan, Jalan Raya Campuan
Hotel: 0361-975368
There is a restaurant ($) in the hotel (▶ 95)
 Penestanan (▶ 61)

55

What to See in Central & West Bali

BALI BARAT, TAMAN NASIONAL ✪✪

Covering over 750sq km, West Bali National Park covers a large portion of the northwestern end of Bali. Entry to the park is from Cekik. There are a number of walking trails (▶ 13), which can only be undertaken with the help of a park guide. There are no restaurants or shops within the park so bring your own food and drinks. Another attraction in the National Park is Pulau Menjangan, a tiny uninhabited island off the northern coast. This island is reached by boat (a half-hour journey) from Labuhan Lalang, which is just to the west of Banyuwedang. Bring your snorkel as the island is deservedly renowned for its coral reefs and the calm sea makes it ideal for beginners. Scuba divers can arrange trips through agents in Kuta.

BALI BOTANICAL GARDENS ✪

Easily located off the main road heading north through Bedugul, the Bali Botanical Gardens (also known as Kebun Raya) were set up in 1959 and have over 600 different species of trees and more than 300 orchids. The large tree at the first roundabout past the entrance is a fine example of a *suku* (podocarp). Unfortunately not everything is labeled in English, but this may change in time. There is a mosque near the gardens and Islamic prayer chants are heard through loudspeakers every Friday – an unusual sound in Bali.

BANGLI ✪✪

The Bangli kingdom was the last one to come under Dutch control (1909) and visitors come to the town of the same name to see the impressive temple of Pura Kehen, handsomely laid out on the terraces of a hillside. The temple's bell tower (*kulkul*) is tucked inside a huge banyan tree in the first courtyard. Also worth seeing is Pura Dalem Pengungekan, a typical temple of the dead adorned with illustrations of the divine retribution awaiting earthly sinners in the next world.

Left: *the open-mouthed face of Bhoma repelling evil from the doors of Pura Kehen*

Right: *the entrance to Goa Gajah may represent Rangda, a legendary widow-witch*

BATUAN ✪

This is another village on the Denpasar to Ubud arts-and-crafts trail. It has given its name to a genre of Balinese painting, characterized by tiny figures and a density of detail, begun in the 1930s when village artists started to experiment with a new style. Today, various styles are available and it takes a while to filter out shops selling tacky reproductions from the genuine galleries.

* 52B1
* 7km south of Ubud
* Denpasar to Ubud *bemos* stop in Batuan
* Ubud's Art Galleries (➤ 24), Sukawati (➤ 46), Mas (➤ 60)

BEDULU ✪

Before the mid-14th century Bedulu was the capital of a powerful empire. Visitors today tend to just drive through on their way to somewhere else, but its 11th-century Pura Samuan Tiga (Temple of the Meeting of the Three), just to the east of the village junction, is a significant reminder of past glories.

* 52B2
* 5km east of Ubud
* *Bemos* between Ubud and Gianyar stop here
* Goa Gajah (➤ 57), Pura Penataran Sasih (➤ 62), Yeh Pulu (➤ 64)

BLAHBATUH ✪

The village of Blahbatuh is famous for its Pura Gaduh temple and in particular a giant carved head that is commonly taken to represent the mythical giant Kebo Iwa. The ancient head is centuries older than the temple itself, which was reconstructed after its destruction in an earthquake in 1917. A sash must be worn.

* 52C1
* 5km southwest of Gianyar
* Pura Gaduh: daily 7–6
* Pura Gaduh: free
* Gianyar (➤ 35), Batuan (➤ 57)

GOA GAJAH ✪

The 'Elephant Cave' is believed to have been built in the 11th century as an abode for Hindu and Buddhist priests, but nowadays it mainly attracts coach tours because of its closeness to Ubud and easy accessibility (it is on the main Ubud–Gianyar road). The entrance to the cave, shaped into the giant mouth of a demon, is far more dramatic and interesting than the interior.

* 52B2
* 5km southeast of Ubud
* Daily 8–5
* Food sold in car park
* Ubud–Gianyar *bemos* stop outside
* Cheap
* Peliatan (➤ 61)

In the Know

If you only have a short time to visit Bali and Lombok, or would like to get a real flavor of the islands, here are some ideas:

Ways To Be A Local

Smile graciously, like the Balinese.

Avoid overt shows of emotion in public.

Always wear a sash when entering a temple.

Dress modestly if attending a temple festival.

Use your car horn frequently to alert other road users to your presence.

Be aware of Muslim sensibilities on the island of Lombok.

Do not discuss religion or Indonesian politics unless you know your company.

Haggle over prices but keep a sense of humor.

Use discretion when taking photographs of people, especially at temple festivals.

Accept the fact that notions of punctuality are quite flexible in Bali and Lombok.

Good Places To Have Lunch

Batu Jimbar ($$), Jalan Danau Tamblingan, Sanur (☎ 0361-287374), on Sanur's main street, is the best place to go for healthy salads and the like.

Biyu-Nasak ($), Lovina Beach (☎ 0362-41176), is Balinese for 'ripe bananas'. Tempting food plus books and magazines to read, and a children's corner.

Bridge Café ($$), Campuan, Ubud (☎ 0361-975085). Try the *blackened ahi* (tuna salad) or *lau-lau* (popular Hawaiian dish).

Café Arma ($$), Ubud (☎ 0361-975742), at the southern end of Jalan Hanoman. A lovely open-air location, with rice paddies behind the restaurant, which serves Italian food.

Kampung Café ($$), Tegallalang, north of Ubud (☎ 0361-901201), has excellent Balinese cooking in a very Ubud setting. Perched on a valley-side overlooking rice terraces, the views are terrific.

La Lucciola ($$), Jalan Oberoi, Seminyak (☎ 0361-730838), is a beachside restaurant in one of Bali's best locations with an excellent Italian-style menu.

Kendedes ($), Padang Bai (☎ 0363-41476), overlooking the ferry port and serving fresh seafood like barracuda and marlin.

Puncak Sari ($), Penelokan (☎ 0366-51073), out of town on the main road to Kintamani. Spectacular views from the outside tables. Lunch buffet and à la carte.

Tirta Ayu ($), Tirtagangga (☎ 0363-21697), inside the Water Palace grounds. Peaceful atmosphere with Indonesian and Western food, including *tahu panggang* (tofu with chips and salad).

Warung Made ($$), Jalan Raya, Seminyak (☎ 0361-732130), is the town's busiest and most famous restaurant with a delicious and diverse menu.

Top Activities

Bird watching: bring binoculars to West Bali National Park and the lakes around Bedugul.

Bungee jumping: take a leap of faith with Bali Bungy Co (☎ 0361-752658) in Kuta. Free transportation within Kuta, Sanur and Nusa Dua area.

Cruising: Bali Hai Cruises (☎ 0361-720331) visit Nusa Lembongan; Spice Cruises (☎ 0361-286283) have three-night adventures to islands east of Lombok.

Diving: Sanur and Candi Dasa in Bali, and Senggigi in Lombok, all have reputable diving operators catering for beginners and professionals.

Golf: Bali Golf & Country Club (☎ 0361-771791) in Nusa Dua or the Bali Handara Kosaido Country Club in Bedugul (➤ 21).

Snorkeling: plenty of snorkeling spots around the coast, gear usually available for hire.

Surfing: the best breaks are in the south of Bali, from April to October.

Suitable for beginners and experts alike.

Swimming: spoilt for choice as regards beaches but always look for designated swimming areas.

Walking: long-distance trails in West Bali National Park. Also in the mountains: Gunung Agung and Gunung Batur in Bali, Gunung Rinjani in Lombok.

Watersports: sailing, windsurfing and other watersports are well-organized activities in Kuta, Sanur, Nusa Dua and Benoa.

Learning to jet ski on Lake Bratan

10
Best Buys

'Antique' furniture of all sizes and descriptions, even made to order!

Batik cloth, sold everywhere and versatile in its uses.

A wood carving in the workshop of an Ubud woodcarver

Clothes, there are numerous boutiques and larger stores selling a wide variety of clothes in Kuta.

Fake designer-name watches in Kuta and Senggigi, but do not expect an international guarantee!

Ikat cloth, produced by a special technique.

Inexpensive arts and crafts sold in Senggigi, Lombok (some of the arts and crafts come from islands further to the east).

Jewelry in Kuta, Ubud and Celuk.

Paintings in Ubud.

Souvenirs such as wind chimes and metal candle holders.

Wood carvings sold in the villages around Ubud and Mas.

10
Things To Avoid

Drinking water from taps.

Driving as if in your home country.

Losing your temper or raising your voice; both actions are viewed as uncouth by the Balinese.

Making eye contact with a street vendor if you don't wish to purchase their wares.

Money changers with calculators that work to your disadvantage (always calculate the sums yourself).

Nude bathing, apart from in the beach resorts in south Bali.

Stepping on the little offerings placed on the pavement by Balinese.

Sunbathing without first applying plenty of sun block.

Swimming outside designated swimming areas on the beach.

Touching people's heads; this action is offensive to Hindus.

59

To reach the workshops of this Peliatan woodcarver takes less than half an hour of walking from central Ubud

GUNUNG KAWI (► 26, TOP TEN)

LAKE BRATAN (► 20, TOP TEN)

MAS   😊😊

Long famous as a woodcarving village, most visitors tend to see only the huge mansions of shops that are set in their own grounds on either side of the 5km stretch of road that runs through Mas. Some of the smaller shops are well worth seeking out. All budgets and tastes are catered for and, while some of the bigger stores have very high-quality products with correspondingly high price-tags, it is still possible to find attractive pieces of art at affordable prices.

MUSEUM PURBAKALA   😊

The archaeological importance of the Pejeng area is considerable (► 61). However, the Museum Purbakala hosts a fairly disappointing collection of finds. Unimpressive examples of Sung- and Yuan-dynasty jars and dishes, and poorly preserved clay stupas from the 8th to 10th centuries, are typical of the artefacts inside the rooms. Outside in the grounds, though, are a group of sarcophagi placed on four sides around a pond and these justify a visit to the museum.

NEGARA   😊

This is the largest town on the west coast and has little to interest visitors except for its annual buffalo racing, which takes place in August and then again around September or October. From Negara the road continues to Gilimanuk at the western tip of Bali but this town, which is a busy port linking Bali with east Java, has even less to attract casual visitors than Negara.

NYUHKUNING   😊😊

This enchanting village area is well worth a visit for its laid-back atmosphere and scattering of shops selling woodcarvings. Set amidst rice fields to the south of Ubud, it can be found by following the track south from the *pura dalem* in the Monkey Forest. The range is less impressive than that found in Mas but prices are more modest. There is also a small woodcarving museum but wandering into one of the woodcarvers' workshops is a far more absorbing experience.

🔲 52B1
✉ 4km south of Ubud
🚌 *Bemos* between Denpasar's Batubulan terminal and Ubud pass through Mas and will stop anywhere along the road
↔ Ubud (► 50–5), Peliatan (► 61)

🔲 52B2
✉ On the right, just after Bedulu, on the road to Tampaksiring
🕐 Mon–Thu 7–2, Fri 7–11, Sat 7–12:30
🍴 Cheap
↔ Bedulu (► 57), Pura Penataran Sasih (► 62), Pura Pusering Jagat (► 62)

🔲 28B3
✉ 95km west of Denpasar
🍴 Best place to eat is at the Wira Pada Hotel ($)
🚌 *Bemos* between Denpasar and Gilimanuk stop in Negara
↔ Rambut Siwi (► 63)

🔲 52B2
✉ 2km south of Ubud
🍴 Pleasant small restaurants ($)
↔ Monkey Forest (► 51)

PEJENG ✪✪

Archaeologists have made important finds in the Pejeng area and the village was once the capital of a kingdom which flourished until the Majapahit invasion in the 14th century. There are three interesting temples, within walking distance of each other, and a small archaeological museum – all are listed in the sidepanel.

🚩 52B2
⊠ 4km east of Ubud
↔ Museum Purbakala
(► 60), Pura Kebo Edan
(► 62), Pura Penataran
Sasih (► 62), Pura
Pusering Jagat (► 62)

PELIATAN ✪✪

Once just a small village famous for its dancers, Peliatan has now merged with the south of Ubud. Jalan Peliatan, the main street in its eastern half, which forms part of the busy route for traffic to and from Denpasar, has the famous Agung Rai art gallery (► 104) and other shops. Apart from shopping, the best reason for being in Peliatan is for a dance performance (► 112), especially one that features the village's all-female gamelan orchestra.

🚩 52B2
⊠ 1.5km southeast of Ubud
🍴 A few small eating places
($) along Jalan Peliatan
↔ Ubud (► 50–5)

PENESTANAN ✪✪✪

Penestanan has more character and appeal than most of the arts-and-crafts villages in the vicinity of Ubud. It is within walking distance of Ubud (steps and a path almost opposite the Hotel Tjampuhan lead to Penestanan) and is well worth considering as a place to stay for a night or two (► 102). The village was home to a renowned school of Balinese art, the Young Artists of the 1960s, and there are a number of modest galleries (► 104) with examples of this style (and of every other style also). With its photogenic scenes of agricultural life and amiable ambiance, Penestanan has managed to retain its rural identity while catering to the needs of tourists. There are restaurants, craft shops, a money changer and even a reasonably good hairdresser! It is a good place in which to wander around and relax.

🚩 52B2
⊠ Less than 2km west of
Ubud
🍴 Pleasant places to eat ($)
↔ Ubud (► 50–5), Walter
Spies' Home (► 55)

Gamelan music is played on a variety of bronze percussion instruments, sometimes accompanied by string and wind instruments

52B2
4km northeast of Ubud
Free
Ubud (➤ 50–5)

PETULU

The attraction here is the awe-inspiring sight of countless thousands of white herons and egrets flying home to roost on the branches of trees each evening. Why the birds have chosen these particular trees in this particular village remains a mystery, but they have been doing so for some thirty years. Arrive well before sunset and afterwards you can stroll beyond the village amid scenes of rural bliss as darkness descends.

52B2
In the village of Pejeng
Daily 8–5
Cheap
Museum Purbakala
(➤ 60), Pejeng (➤ 61),
Pura Penataran Sasih
(➤ 62), Pura Pusering
Jagat (➤ 62)
A sash must be worn

PURA KEBO EDAN

This temple (known also as the Crazy Buffalo temple) has acquired a certain notoriety due to its huge statue of a god or man and his equally huge penis. According to one interpretation the figure boasts six penises, though no one knows quite why, and there is equal uncertainty about the identity of the giant figure itself. To add to the mystery – what exactly is the significance of the apparently female figure that the dancing giant tramples on?

52B2
In the village of Pejeng
Daily 8–5
Cheap
Museum Purbakala
(➤ 60), Pejeng (➤ 61),
Pura Kebo Edan (➤ 62),
Pura Pusering Jagat
(➤ 62)
A sash must be worn

PURA PENATARAN SASIH

This was the state temple for the Pejeng kingdom but its present claim to fame is to be found inside the inner courtyard. A 3m bronze drum, said to be the largest kettledrum in the world, is at least one thousand years old and carries with it a strange tale. The story goes that it fell from the sky like a fallen moon and landed in a tree. Its brightness hindered the work of thieves, one of whom urinated on it in disgust only to be killed in an ensuing explosion that saw the moon fall to the ground as a drum.

52B2
In the village of Pejeng
Daily 8–5
Cheap
Museum Purbakala
(➤ 60), Pejeng (➤ 61),
Pura Kebo Edan (➤ 62),
Pura Penataran Sasih
(➤ 62)
A sash must be worn

PURA PUSERING JAGAT

A 14th-century sandstone water-carrier is the attraction at this otherwise standard temple. Balinese couples come here for another reason; the temple is regarded as a source of fertility.

Did you know ?

Balinese temples may seem to come in all shapes and sizes but they adhere to a basic plan enshrined by tradition. There are three courtyards, divided by low walls and gateways, with the holiest being the inner one that houses the main shrines. All temples have open-sided, usually thatched, pavilions (bale) and graceful multi-tiered shrines (meru) that always have an odd number of levels. The higher the number (from three to eleven) the more prestigious is the god being honored.

The 11-roofed meru *of Pura Ulun Danu Bratan is dedicated to Vishnu*

PURA ULUN DANU BRATAN ✪✪

This scenic temple dates back to 1633, when it was built under the orders of the king of Mengwi and dedicated to Dewi Danu (Goddess of Water). The Balinese consider the lake to be home to the goddess. The temple's striking position, projecting into the lake, almost caused its downfall in the 1970s when the lake water began to rise unexpectedly. The gardens adjoining the temple are very pleasant and ideal for a picnic.

RAMBUT SIWI ✪

Rambut Siwi is situated about 4km east of Mendaya on the coast road that heads to the west end of Bali. Given its cliff top location overlooking a beach, it should come as no surprise to learn it was founded by the priest Nirartha, who also established Tanah Lot (➤ 47) and Uluwatu (➤ 26). Some of Nirartha's hair is said to reside in one of the shrines in the inner courtyard.

SANGEH MONKEY FOREST ✪

The forest has a legendary connection with the Hindu epic *Ramayana* for it is said that Rama's general, Hanuman, tried to kill the enemy by dropping a piece of mountain – complete with a band of his monkeys – on them at Sangeh. To say that the monkeys are mischievous is an understatement; watch your belongings. There is a temple, Pura Bukit Sari, in the middle of the forest with an ancient statue of a *garuda* (half-human/half-bird creature from Hindu mythology).

✚	28D3
✉	Lake Bratan, Bedugul
☎	0368-21191
⏱	Daily 8–5
🍽	Tourist restaurant ($)
✋	Cheap
↔	Lake Bratan (➤ 20), Bali Botanical Gardens (➤ 56), Taman Rekreasi Bedugul (➤ 64)

✚	28B3
✉	30km west of Soka
⏱	Daily 8–5
🚌	*Bemos* between Denpasar and Gilimanuk will stop at the turnoff ending at the temple
✋	Cheap

✚	52A2
✉	In Sangeh, 21km north of Denpasar
⏱	Daily 8–6
🚌	*Bemos* run direct to Sangeh from Denpasar
✋	Cheap

TAMAN BURUNG

See 'Culture and Wildlife' (► 111) for details of the Bali Bird Park (Taman Burung).

TAMAN REKREASI BEDUGUL

The Bedugul Leisure Park (Taman Rekreasi) is on the right side of the road as you enter Bedugul from the south. The quietest activity is to hire a canoe and paddle to the lakeside temple of Pura Ulun Danu Bratan but there are also motorized water sports, like jet-skiing, on offer.

🚻 29D3
✉ Bedugul
🕐 Daily 8–6
🍴 A couple of restaurants ($) in Bedugul
🚌 Bemos traveling between Singaraja and southern Bali stop in Bedugul
✋ Cheap
↔ Lake Bratan (► 20), Bali Botanical Gardens (► 56), Pura Ulun Danu Bratan (► 63)

Bedugal Leisure Park is on the southern shores of Lake Bratan

TIRTA EMPUL

The holy springs at the Tirta Empul temple have been used by the Balinese since the 10th century. This is not surprising given the legend that the waters contain the spirit of immortality after the spring's creation by the god Indra. The temple and spring complex have been renovated a number of times and the place is well geared to receiving Balinese believers as well as tourists. Tirta Empul is off the main Kintamani–Tampaksiring road, just north of the turn-off to Gunung Kawi.

🚻 29E3
✉ 17km north of Ubud
🕐 Daily 7–6
🍴 Foodstalls ($) near the entrance
🚌 Bemos traveling between Kintamani and Tampaksiring will stop at the turn-off for Tirta Empul
✋ Cheap
↔ Gunung Kawi (► 26)

YEH PULU ⭐⭐

Although the Yeh Pulu rock carvings are near Ubud, surprisingly few visitors seek them out. It is well worth the effort of coming to see the intriguing 14th-century figures cut from the rock face. There may be a narrative link to the panels or perhaps they are just scenes of everyday life. The second panel on the left shows an elegant woman alongside a man carrying wine jars on a pole. The next panel shows a seated woman alongside a farmer, with other figures to the sides. Other panels show a hunting group attacking a boar, and then boars being carried away on a pole. Another scene shows a woman apparently trying to hold back a hunter on horseback, or is she being pulled along? Yeh Pulu can be combined with a trip to nearby Goa Gajah.

🚻 52B2
✉ 1.5km southeast of Goa Gajah, signposted
🕐 Daily 7–6
🍴 Made's Café ($) is next to the ticket office
✋ Cheap
↔ Goa Gajah (► 57)

A Shopping Drive from Ubud

Depart from Ubud and take the main road south to Denpasar through Peliatan. After about 3km there is a right turn signposted for Denpasar. Ignore this and go straight on.

As well as passing woodcarvers at work by the side of the road, you will come across a large upmarket art gallery, Nyoman Sumerta, and after 1.5km The Duck Man (► 107). A little further down this road is the entrance to Goa Gajah (► 57). A sign points the way to Yeh Pulu (► 64) further along the road.

Carry on for 2.5km and turn right, signposted Denpasar.

You will drive past the village of Kutri and its temple.

Carry on to Blahbatuh (► 57) where a diversion can be taken by turning left for Bona.

The shops in the village of Bona are dedicated to bamboo and other woven products: wind chimes, furniture, lampshades, baskets. From Bona return to Blahbatuh.

At Blahbatuh turn right for Denpasar (straight on if returning from Bona) and look for a sign on the left for the Waterfall Restaurant, 1.5km down a side road.

This is a good place for lunch as the view overlooks a waterfall where bungee jumps occur throughout the day.

Once back on the main road it is less than 2km to the next junction. Turn right for Mas (► 60) and Ubud.

The first shop worth stopping at, the Pantheon Gallery (► 106), is on the left, while further along the road is the smaller but smart Villa Interiors (► 106). There are plenty of other shops in Mas to delay your return to Ubud.

Distance
20km

Time
Up to 8 hours, depending on stops

Start/end point
Ubud
✚ 52B2

Lunch
Waterfall Restaurant ($$)
✉ Tegenungan, Kemenuh
☎ 0361-299265

The proprietor-to-be of an Ubud craft shop awaits your custom

65

North & East Bali

The north and east of Bali offers quite a different experience to that provided by the central and southern regions. Although it was in the north that the Dutch established their capital, the area now seems more Balinese and less touristy than the south. This is despite the growing popularity of the Lovina beach area, once a budget traveler's hideout but now catering to everyone while retaining its relaxing and low-key appeal. It is a place where people tend to stay longer than they planned to, deterred from leaving by relatively lower expenses and the hospitable nature of a corner of Bali that remains uncrowded. The place that is overrun with visitors, and understandably so, is the volcanic Gunung Batur area in the northeast. A breathtaking caldera with a spectacular lake is one of the most impressive sights anywhere in Bali.

> *'Lo, from the pasanggrahan we beheld the valley with its blue lake alongside the lava-blackened slopes of the death-dealing volcano, which belched brimstone from its three craters.'*

FRANK CLURE
To the Isles of Spice (1940)

Facing page: *rice fields, Pupuan*

Singaraja

The Dutch made Singaraja their headquarters for ruling Bali and the first waves of tourists to the island all disembarked here from their cruise ships. The Japanese also based themselves here during World War II, but after the war the focus shifted to the more heavily populated south. Today, Singaraja is still the largest city outside of Denpasar and, although most visitors tend to pass through it on their way to Lovina, it deserves a closer look.

The tourist office (✉ 0362-41161) is south of town at 23 Jalan Veteran and very close to Gedong Kirtya (➤ 69) and Puri Sinar Nadi Putri (➤ 69). The town's large new temple, Pura Agung Jagatnata, is 2km to the north. It is close to the commercial heart of the city and the main thoroughfare, Jalan Jen Achmad Yani, which runs east–west and out to Lovina. Banks, shops, restaurants and a post office are all located along Jalan Jen Achmad Yani and the old harbor area is just 500m to the north. Singaraja is worth visiting simply for the experience of a Balinese town that is not catering to tourism. At night there is little to detain a visitor except perhaps a stroll around the night market which is located around Jalan Durian, opposite the main junction where Jalan Jen Achmad Yani meets Jalan Gajah Mada.

An arresting view from the Singaraja road

What to See in Singaraja

GEDONG KIRTYA

This library has a unique collection of some 3,000 manuscripts inscribed on the leaves of the *lontar* palm. This is the only library of its kind in the world and, though established and maintained for scholars, it is open to the public. The texts are mostly written in Balinese or in Javanese script and cover subjects like religion, astrology and traditional medicine.

🕂 29D4
✉ 20 Jalan Veteran
🕐 Mon–Thu 8–2, Fri 8–11
💷 Cheap

Patience and skill go into preparing the lontar palms and engraving the text on to them

HARBOUR AND WATERFRONT ✪

The harbor is now little used, with little to suggest its former importance apart from empty warehouses. At the entrance there is an eye-catching monument, built in 1987, commemorating an incident during the struggle for independence in the 1940s when a Balinese was killed by gunfire from a Dutch vessel. There is a small Chinese temple nearby.

🕂 29D4
✉ Jalan Erlangga

PURA AGUNG JAGATNATA ✪

This is a surprising temple simply because it is so new, dating back merely to 1993. It is more likely to be closed than open, but look for the giant elephant-headed figure of Ganesh on the outside of the temple.

🕂 29D4
✉ Jalan Pramuka
🕐 Irregular hours
🍴 Gandi restaurant ($)
(▶ 98)

PURI SINAR NADI PUTRI

This is a small, inconspicuous weaving factory, easy to miss completely because the entrance is up a lane just to the left of the entrance to the Gedong Kirtya (see above). Visitors are welcome to wander in and are likely to be shown the foot-operated looms clattering and clunking away. All the machines are operated by women and the *ikat* cloth they produce is made by leaving the warp threads (those running lengthwise) undyed while the weft threads (those running across the warp) receive the dye. There is a small room with a modest selection on sale.

🕂 29D4
✉ Jalan Veteran
🕐 Daily 8–4
💷 Free

What to See in North & East Bali

AMED ✪✪✪

29F3
⊠ 18km north of Amlapura
🍴 Many along the coast road ($)
↔ Wreck of the *Liberty* (► 76)

Amed, once a sleepy east-coast fishing village, offers spectacular views of Gunung Agung (► 17). The black-sand beach is home to a small fleet of local fishing boats and is the workplace for salt-panners. There are numerous cheap but excellent accommodations and restaurants.

BANJAR TEGA HOT SPRINGS ✪✪

28C3
⊠ 10km southwest of Lovina
🕐 Daily 8–6
🍴 Komala Tirta restaurant ($)
🎫 Cheap
↔ Brahma Vihara Ashrama (► 72)

Bring swimming gear and a bar of soap (soap is only allowed in one of the pools) and enjoy a soak in the *air panas* (hot springs). These pools, at Banjar, are well maintained, changing rooms and toilets are provided, and there are a number of small shops close by selling souvenirs, spices (► 106), and fabrics. Only at weekends do the hot springs become crowded.

BESAKIH ✪✪

28E3
⊠ 60km northeast of Denpasar
🕐 Daily 8–5
🍴 Several tourist restaurants ($) outside the complex
🚌 *Bemos* from Klungkung
🎫 Cheap
↔ Gunung Agung (► 17)

Dramatically situated about 1,000m up the slopes of Gunung Agung, this is the holiest of all temple sites in Bali. The founder is said to be an 8th-century Javanese priest; however the site may well go back to prehistoric times. There are 22 temples, dominated by the large Pura Penataran Agung, spread out over nearly 3km. Only

devotees are allowed to enter the temples but some of the splendor of Pura Penataran Agung may still be appreciated from the outside. Despite the terrifying power of Gunung Agung's eruption in 1963, the Besakih temple complex was not destroyed. Priests are said to have thrown themselves into the flames in acts of desperate appeasement, and most of the post-eruption work involved restoration rather than rebuilding. Try to arrive as early in the morning as possible to beat the crowds.

This temple umbrella adorns one of the 22 temples in the Besakih complex

A Countryside Walk

This walk begins just off the main coast road, 10km west of Lovina, where there is a large stone arch across the road that heads inland to Banjar Tega Hot Springs and Brahma Vihara Ashrama. Catch any west-bound *bemo* from Lovina or, with your own transport, park off the main road.

Scenes of rural bliss encountered on a countryside walk west of Lovina

Walk inland for a little less than 1.5km and then turn left at the junction.

At this junction inexpensive rides on the back of a motorbike may be hired as an alternative to a pleasant, though uphill, 7km walk to the next junction.

On arrival at this next junction take the right turn (signposted) to the Brahma Vihara Ashrama monastery (► 72).

The final 1km walk to the monastery passes through a bougainvillea-lined village with fighting cocks caged in their baskets along the sides of homes. The monastery has a delightful hillside location and there is a small shop close by selling fresh mangoes to quench a thirst.

From the monastery retrace your steps to the junction (8km) where the motorbike rides are hired and turn left. After less than 500m, turn left again for the hot springs (air panas) at the signposted junction that points the way.

This stretch of road crosses a small river and passes through a village where there is always something to catch the eye, whether it be children taking the family goat for a walk or baskets of grapes for local wine production. At Banjar Tega Hot Springs(► 70) enjoy a bath and a meal.

Finally head back to the main coast road (a walk of 3km).

Distance
8km (16km if a motorbike ride is not hired)

Time
3–4 hours with a motorbike ride

Start/end point
10km west of Lovina on the coast road
✚ 29C3

Lunch
Komala Tirta Restaurant ($)
✉ Banjar Tega Hot Springs

The lotus pond at Brahma Vihara Ashrama is surrounded by 12 statues

BRAHMA VIHARA ASHRAMA ✪✪

This beautiful Buddhist monastery, built in 1972 and repaired after earthquake damage four years later, is unique to Bali and was built with help from Thailand. Just inside the entrance there is a fountain in a lotus pond with 12 statues around it. The whole place has a wonderfully serene atmosphere. As with Hindu temples, it is obligatory to wear a sash and these can be borrowed when making a donation to the monastery.

GUNUNG AGUNG (➤ 17, TOP TEN)

GUNUNG BATUR AND LAKE BATUR (➤ 18–19, TOP TEN)

JAGARAGA ✪✪

The Dutch attacked and took Jagaraga in 1849 and the impact of their colonialism has been famously recorded in the stone of the village's *pura dalem* (temple of the dead). The front wall of the temple has an engaging set of panels depicting Balinese life before and after the Dutch. The pre-colonial days are represented by carvings of the climbing of coconut trees and the catching of huge fish, followed by panels showing the Dutch arriving by road and air. On the right side of the entrance the most notable panel is that of two Dutch men in their car being surrounded by Balinese robbers.

LOVINA ✪✪✪

Lovina is the collective name for a beach-resort area strung out along the coast to the west of Singaraja that includes more than one village. Partly because of Lovina's 8km

---

✚ 28C3
✉ 10km southwest of Lovina
🕐 Daily 7–6
👐 Cheap
↔ Banjar Tega Hot Springs (➤ 70)
❓ The monastery may be visited as part of a walk (➤ 71)

✚ 29D4
✉ 9km southeast of Singaraja
🚌 *Bemos* from Singaraja
👐 Free
↔ Pura Bejit Sangsit (➤ 74), Pura Dalem Sangsit (➤ 74), Pura Meduwe Karang (➤ 75)

✚ 28C3
✉ 10km west of Singaraja
🍴 Many restaurants ($–$$)

stretch there is little sense of overcrowding but nonetheless the area is growing in popularity all the time. There is an excellent range of restaurants, mostly dotted along the coast road and offering views of unforgettable sunsets from tables close to the beach (▶ 97). Accommodation used to be mainly budget places but more and more mid-range hotels with air-conditioning and swimming pools are opening (▶ 103).

A concentration of visitor facilities has developed around the village of Kalibukbuk, including a small Tourist Information office, money changers and places to hire cars, motorbikes and bicycles. The black-sand beach of Lovina is generally safe for swimming and while it is possible to snorkel directly off the beach, it is equally easy to arrange trips by boat. Diving is possible for both beginners and those already qualified but there is no scope for surfing. Dolphin watching is another favorite activity, beginning around 6AM when you board a *prahu* (traditional Indonesian boat with bamboo stabilizers). Nightlife is fairly quiet, although pubs and bars are springing up and some restaurants offer a dance show or video film.

🍴 Many restaurants ($–$$)

↔ Banjar Tega Hot Springs (▶ 70), Brahma Vihara Ashrama (▶ 72)

❓ Information from Singaraja tourist office (☎ 0362-41161) or Kalibukbuk tourist office (🕐 Mon–Thu 7–5, Fri 7–1, Sat 7–5 – shares premises with the village police station)

PENELOKAN ⭐⭐
The word *penelokan* means 'place to look' and the village has grown on the strength of its ability to offer unparalleled views of a stupendous landscape. Lake Batur, with Gunung Batur on one side and the smaller Gunung Abang on the other, looks truly majestic on a clear day. The only drawback is the location's popularity and the inevitable hordes of hawkers.

🔲 29E3

✉ 60km north of Denpasar

🍴 Tourist restaurants ($–$$)

🚌 *Bemos* running between Denpasar and Kintamani stop in Penelokan

PUPUAN ⭐
Visitors to Pupuan are invariably passing through on their way to or from Seririt on the north coast. The road is a winding and demanding route across mountains, so everyone except the driver enjoys the magnificent scenery all around. At Pupuan there is a waterfall but the real appeal is the views of the surrounding valleys and hills.

🔲 28C3

✉ 42km southwest of Singaraja

Sunset from Lovina

73

A detail from a carving in pink sandstone in Pura Beji Sangsit

<table>
<tr><td>✚</td><td>29D4</td></tr>
<tr><td>✉</td><td>7km east of Singaraja, near Sangsit village</td></tr>
<tr><td>🕐</td><td>Daily 8–5</td></tr>
<tr><td>🚌</td><td>Bemos run east along the coast road from Singaraja</td></tr>
<tr><td></td><td>Cheap</td></tr>
<tr><td>↔</td><td>Pura Dalem Sangsit (▶ 74)</td></tr>
<tr><td>❓</td><td>A sash must be worn</td></tr>
</table>

PURA BEJI SANGSIT

It is easy to miss this temple (look for a black-and-blue sign on the north side of the coastal road about 8km east of Singaraja) but it is worth seeking out for the lively energy of its carvings. The exterior panels display some brilliant examples of *nagas* (snake-like creatures) while the gateways into the middle and inner courtyards have a rich profusion of other mythical creatures. As it is dedicated to agricultural spirits, this is known as a *subak* temple. A *subak* is an association of rice farmers sharing a water supply and working together to irrigate their land.

<table>
<tr><td>✚</td><td>29D4</td></tr>
<tr><td>✉</td><td>7km east of Singaraja, near Sangsit village</td></tr>
<tr><td>🕐</td><td>Daylight hours</td></tr>
<tr><td>🚌</td><td>Bemos run east along the coast road from Singaraja</td></tr>
<tr><td>✋</td><td>Free</td></tr>
<tr><td>↔</td><td>Pura Beji Sangsit (▶ 74)</td></tr>
</table>

PURA DALEM SANGSIT

This temple of the dead can be seen from the road in front of Pura Beji Sangsit and it is reached by threading one's way along the paths between the intervening rice fields and jumping over the occasional water channel. The far left corner of the front wall of the temple has a carved scene of sexual bliss, while the wall to the right of the entrance depicts the horrors of hell. There are other grotesque stone creatures inside the temple and fun can be had trying to determine the nature of some of the pictorial carvings.

<table>
<tr><td>✚</td><td>29F3</td></tr>
<tr><td>✉</td><td>7km northeast of Tirtagangga</td></tr>
<tr><td>↔</td><td>Tirtagangga (▶ 22)</td></tr>
</table>

PURA LEMPUYANG LUHUR ✪

Visiting this temple is very good exercise as it takes about two hours to climb up to it through the forested side of a mountain; the route is signposted from the village of Abang. Upon reaching the summit of Gunung Lempuyang the temple itself may prove to be a little anticlimactic but there is ample compensation afforded by the panoramic view of Gunung Agung. There are places to rest along the route to the top but bring plenty of water and something to eat.

PURA MEDUWE KARANG ✪✪✪

Just past the turn-off for the Kintamani road on the coastal road, 12km east from Singaraja, this is another temple dedicated to the gods of agriculture but, unlike Pura Beji Sangsit, it concerns itself only with dry crops. Many visitors come here to see one particularly famous and much-photographed panel carving, that of a man on a bicycle with flower petal wheels (one of which is about to run over a rat) being pursued by a dog. It can be found at the bottom of the main block in the inner courtyard and it is thought possible that the man, who doesn't look Balinese, is the Dutch artist Nieuwenkamp who traveled around by bicycle in the early years of the 20th century.

🔢 29D4
✉ 12km east of Singaraja, in the village of Kubutambahan
🕐 Daily 8–5
🚌 Bemos run east along the coast road from Singaraja
💵 Cheap
↔ Jagaraga (➤ 72), Pura Beji Sangsit (➤ 74), Pura Dalem Sangsit (➤ 74)
❓ A sash must be worn

PURA ULUN DANU BATUR ✪✪

An eruption of Gunung Batur in 1926 destroyed the village of Batur and its temple. The community responded by moving up to the crater rim and rebuilding their village and the temple. The temple's importance is reflected in the fact that the *meru* (multi-roofed shrine) has 11 roofed sections, the highest possible number. The temple is also unusual in having extra courtyards adjoining the three conventional ones. The extra space is needed for the annual *odalan* festival (➤ 116). Most unusual of all, the temple is served by young males selected by a priestess. The senior male priest has an ambassadorial role for the goddess of the lake to whom the temple is dedicated.

🔢 29E3
✉ 2km south of Kintamani
🕐 Daily 8–5
🚌 *Bemos* to or from Singaraja
💵 Cheap
↔ Gunung Batur and Lake Batur (➤ 18–19), Penelokan (➤ 73)
❓ A sash must be worn

TIRTAGANGGA (➤ 22, TOP TEN)

The carvings of Pura Meduwe Karang are a highlight of any visit to the north of Bali

75

29E3

✉ East side of Lake Batur

🚢 Boats depart regularly from Kedisan between 8AM and 4PM. The boat ride is 1 hour each way

🥾 Boat ride: moderate

↔ Gunung Batur and Lake Batur (▶ 18–19)

TRUNYAN ✪

The village of Trunyan is inhabited by the Bali Aga, the original Balinese, whose culture predates the Majapahit takeover of the 14th century. There is a footpath from Abang to the village or you may prefer to go by boat from Kedisan. A little beyond the village is the Trunyan cemetery at Kuban, famous because the villagers do not bury or cremate their dead but expose them to the air where the bodies decompose over time. The recently dead are covered up by what is effectively a bamboo coffin. The cemetery is only accessible by boat from Kedisan and many visitors find the whole experience to be a tourist trap.

29F3

✉ 35m off the beach at Tulamben, 27km north of Amlapura

🍴 Modest choice of restaurants ($)

🚌 Bemos from Amlapura and Singaraja

↔ Amed (▶ 70)

WRECK OF THE *LIBERTY* ✪✪

The *Liberty* was a US cargo ship that survived World War I only to be badly damaged by Japanese torpedoes in 1942 and consequently beached off the eastern coast of Bali near Tulamben village. The eruption of Gunung Agung in 1963 caused the ship to break up and sink into deeper water, and the wreck is now a very popular diving site. It is close enough to the beach to be reached by snorkelers who can glimpse some of the colorful fish inhabiting the coral-encrusted wreck.

The beauty of diving the Liberty wreck is that it can be accessed directly from the beach

29D4

✉ 15km east of Singaraja

🚌 Bemos along coast road

🕐 Daily 7–7

🍴 At Puri Sanih hotel ($)

🥾 Springs: cheap

↔ Pura Beji Sangsit (▶ 74), Pura Dalem Sangsit (▶ 74), Pura Meduwe Karang (▶ 75)

YEH SANIH ✪✪

Yeh Sanih, also known as Air Sanih, is a modest beach resort to the east of Singaraja on Bali's relatively untouched northern coast. Its attractions are cold freshwater springs very close to the sea, but set in landscaped grounds with their own changing rooms. There is a small hotel and restaurant next door. Yeh Sanih makes a pleasant overnight stop while exploring the coastline and there is a temple, Pura Taman Manik Mas, 7km further east along the main road.

A Drive from Singaraja to Lake Batur

This drive begins in Singaraja and finishes in Penelokan.

Start from Singaraja and drive eastwards along the coastal road. After 8km a faded black-and-blue sign on the left of the road points to Pura Beji Sangsit (▶ 74). Drive 200m down the indicated sideroad.

After visiting Pura Beji Sangsit, it is a short walk to Pura Dalem Sangsit (▶ 74).

Return to the main road and continue east for 600m. Look for a sign pointing inland to Jagaraga. (Do not take the narrow lane on the right which the sign seems to be pointing to; the actual turning is 100m further along the road.)

Drive south to Jagaraga (▶ 72). The village's main attraction is the *pura dalem* (temple of the dead) with curious façade bas-reliefs depicting Dutch colonists, aeroplanes, cars and bicycles. After your visit, return once again to the main coastal road.

Continue east along the coastal road for 4km, until reaching the junction at Kubutambahan.

Just beyond this junction, on the coast road, Pura Meduwe Karang (▶ 75) may be visited and Yeh Sanih (▶ 76) lies beyond that.

At Kubutambahan take the inland road south to Kintamani.

About 7km before Kintamani, you will pass Pura Tegeh Koripan temple, and 2km after Kintamani is Pura Ulun Danu Batur (▶ 75). From here it's not far to Penelokan (▶ 73) and the panoramic views of Lake Batur and Gunung Batur.

Distance
42km

Time
5–7 hours, depending on places visited

Start point
Singaraja
✚ 29D4

End point
Penelokan
✚ 29E3

Lunch
Puncak Sari ($) (▶ 98)
✉ Just over 2km before Penelokan on the left side of road
☎ 0366-51073

Penelokan, which translates as 'place to look' deserves its name with views like this of Lake Batur

77

Lombok

Lombok is not Bali. Only 35km separate the two islands but they differ in a number of important respects. The further east one travels in Lombok the more noticeable the different physical landscape becomes. The land is dry and bush-like, with corn and sago often grown instead of rice. Only the north of Lombok has the lushness of Bali, hence the saying 'you can see Bali in Lombok, but not Lombok in Bali'. The indigenous people, the Sasaks, are Muslims and only in the more-developed tourist locations are they becoming as familiarized to visitors as the Balinese. This, of course, is part of Lombok's appeal. The island receives only a fraction of the number of visitors that Bali gets each year and although there are ambitious plans to develop the tourist infrastructure, Lombok still feels like an unexplored island.

> *'The remarkable change ... at the Straits of Lombock* [sic]*, separating the island of that name from Bali; and which is at once so large in amount and of so fundamental a character as to form an important feature in the zoological geography of our globe.'*

ALFRED RUSSEL WALLACE
The Malay Archipelago (1869)

————————●————————

Facing page: *a young Sasak girl*

LOMBOK

Laut Bali

Makassar
(Ujungpandang)

0   10   20 km

3

Lokokrangan · Segenter · **Anyar**

Bayan

Obelobel

Senaru · Belanting · Gili Lawang

Gili · Sidanggala · Sembalun · Gili Sulat

Gili Trawangan · Meno · Gili Air · Gondang · Waterfall · Lawang

Tiuteja · Sambelia

Tanjung · Waterfall · Labuhanpandan · Gili

Sira · Bangsal · *Segara* · *3726 m* · Pentangan

Pemenang · *Anak* · ▲ *Gunung* · ▲ *2330m*

Monkey Forest · *Rinjani* · *Gn. Nangi*

Mangsit · L O M B O K · Pesugulan

Senggigi · **Pura** · Poto

Selat Lombok · **Batubolong** · Sesaot · Tano

Gunungsari · Waterfall · **Labuhan** · Pulau

Pura Segara · Tetebatu · **lombok** · Belang

Ampenan · **Cakranegara** · Kotaraja · Aikmel · Pringgabaya

MATARAM · Sweta · Narmada · Uoyok · Masbagik

Gunung Pengsong · Kediri · Ubung · Kopang · Sikur · **Selong**

Temple · Sukarara · **Praya** · Janapria · Sakra · **Labuhan**

Padangbai, Bali (3.5 hr.) · Gerung · Penujak · Batunyale · Mujur · Keruak · **Haji**

Lembar · *716 m* · Sengkol · **Fish**

2

Bangko- · Gili · Sekotong · **Traditional** · **Market**

bangko · Gede · Tengah · **Sasak Village** · Sade

418 m · Pelangan · *Selong* · Sengkol · **Selat Alas**

Blanak · **Nyale Ritual** · Ekas · Tanjung

1

Padangbai, · *Beach* · Kuta · Ringgit

Bali · *Batu* · **SUMBAWA**

Rujaan

A   B   C

Ampenan-Mataram-Cakranegara-Sweta

Not so much the main city on Lombok as a sprawling conurbation spreading eastwards for 8km, engulfing four once-separate towns. One main road, with multiple changes of name, connects the four towns and *bemos* shuttle regularly between them. Although the airport and the seaport are nearby many visitors only skirt the towns.

The main tourist office for Lombok (🕐 Mon–Sat 7–2, ☎ 0370-31730) is at 70 Jalan Langko at the eastern end of Ampenan. Ampenan has the island's museum and a Balinese temple, and Jalan Yos Sudarso has shops selling arts and crafts from islands to the east of Lombok. Mataram is an administrative center with little appeal for visitors, but Cakranegara was the island's capital when Balinese influence was at its height in the 18th century and a water palace and a temple remain as a legacy of that era. Cakranegara is also a good place to find somewhere to eat and the top floor of the Mataram Plaza on Jalan Pejanggik has a number of inexpensive food outlets. The town of Sweta forms the eastern end of the conurbation and functions as Lombok's transport capital. Close to the busy bus station there is a large covered market area that is worth a visit.

Ampenan may seem hectic and urban but quiet spots are not difficult to find (left)

Horse-drawn carts, called cidemos, may be hired for short journeys in Lombok (below)

Typical Balinese architecture from the Mayura Water Palace

What to See in Ampenan–Mataram–Cakranegara–Sweta

MAYURA WATER PALACE ✪✪

Built in the mid-18th century, Mayura Water Palace (also known as Puri Mayura) was the seat of power for the Balinese kingdom that ruled western Lombok at that time. Its appearance may surprise visitors as this 'palace' consists of an artificial lake set in an attractive park, with a raised path leading to a pavilion in the middle of the lake. This pavilion was where justice was meted out under the Balinese kingdom.

PURA MERU ✪

This early 18th-century temple is the largest in Lombok and was built for Prince Anak Agung Made Karang – more for political than religious reasons – in an attempt to unite the various Hindu groups on the island. After entering, turn left to reach the inner courtyard and its three *meru* (multi-roofed shrines). They represent three mountains: Bromo in Java, Rinjani in Lombok and Agung in Bali.

PURA SEGARA ✪

This red-and-white Balinese temple is close to the beach north of Ampenan. It is usually locked but just to the northeast is an old Chinese cemetery that is worth wandering over to. The dirt-track approach road passes through a small settlement which is a sad reminder of the poverty in which many islanders live.

WEST NUSA TENGGARA PROVINCIAL MUSEUM ✪✪

This makes a useful introduction to some aspects of Lombok life. There are paintings of traditional dress and lifestyle, various objects and artefacts from working life, ceramics, musical instruments, shadow puppets, krises (Indonesian daggers with wavy blades), and displays on flora and fauna. A museum guidebook is available in English.

🚩 80A2
✉ Jalan Selaparang, Cakranegara
🕐 Daily 8–4:30 💰 Cheap
↔ Pura Meru (▶ below)

🚩 80A2
✉ Off Jalan Selaparang, Cakranegara
🕐 Daily 8–5
💰 Cheap
↔ Mayura Water Palace (▶ above)
❓ A sash must be worn

🚩 80A2
✉ Off Jalan Saleh Sunkar, Ampenan
🕐 Odd hours, often locked
↔ West Nusa Tenggara Provincial Museum (▶ below)

🚩 80A2
✉ Jalan Panji Tilar Negara, Ampenan
☎ 0370-32159
🕐 Tue–Sun 8–3
↔ Pura Segara (▶ above)
💰 Cheap

What to See in Lombok

BAYAN ✪

The mosque in this small Sasak village on the north coast is regarded as Lombok's oldest, dating back over 300 years, and Bayan may have been the first village to convert to Islam. This village is also the starting point favored by many attempting to climb Gunung Rinjani (► below).

☩ 80B3
✉ 60km northeast of Ampenan
🚌 *Bemos* from Sweta
↔ Segenter (► 88), Senaru (► 88)

GILI ISLANDS (► 21, TOP TEN)

GUNUNG PENGSONG ✪✪

It takes half an hour of climbing steep steps (from the temple complex at the bottom) to reach the top of Gunung Pengsong, but the reward is a rich, panoramic view of the surrounding countryside, the sea and Gunung Rinjani (► below) in the distance. It helps to set off early in the morning, before clouds set in, to catch sight of Gunung Agung (► 17) in Bali. An important harvest festival takes place each year around April. At the summit there is a small Hindu shrine.

☩ 80A2
✉ 6km south of Mataram
↔ Ampenan-Mataram-Cakranegara-Sweta (► 81)

GUNUNG RINJANI ✪✪✪

This is the highest mountain in Lombok (3,726m), the third highest in Indonesia, and is still an active volcano. The mountain is revered by both Sasaks and Balinese, and full moon brings them to the crater rim or the lake to pray and make offerings. During an annual *Pakelem* ceremony, a traditional practice is to throw gifts of gold jewelry into the lake. Do not attempt to climb Rinjani without a guide (available in Bayan) and although there are shelters on the mountain, climbers should bring a tent, or at least a sleeping bag, if intending to stay overnight. The reward is a view of the stunning colors of Segara Anak (Child of the Sea) Lake, and the temptation to spend another day descending to the lake and bathing in the hot springs.

☩ 80B2
✉ 30km west of Senggigi
🍴 Bring your own food and drink
🚌 *Bemos* from Sweta to Bayan, then take a *bemo* to Senaru

The Lombok countryside from the summit of Gunung Pengsong

⊕ 80B1
⊠ 60km south of Ampenan
🍴 Use the restaurants ($) of
   nearby hotels
🚌 Bemos from Praya

*Kuta beach in south
Lombok – an endless,
empty stretch of white
sand*

⊕ 80C2
⊠ 74km east of Ampenan
🚌 Bemos from Sweta
⛴ Ferry to Poto Tano on
   Sumbawa

⊕ 80A1
⊠ 22km south of Ampenan
🚌 Bemos to Sweta

KUTA   ✪✪✪

Not to be confused with Bali's famous Kuta beach,
Lombok's Kuta is developing as a new resort area along the
island's southern coast. The tourist infrastructure is modest
but that will change in time. For the moment, however,
Kuta is a quiet, peaceful retreat set amid stunning coastal
scenery. Legend has it that a local princess drowned
herself here after being forced to choose a husband; an
annual mid-February festival commemorates the event. A
short drive to the east will bring you to Aan Beach, with its
spectacular double bay. Equidistant to the west is Mawun
Bay, one of Lombok's prettiest.

LABUHAN LOMBOK   ✪✪

This is the ferry port for the sparsely populated island of
Sumbawa but there is nothing else to attract the visitor.
The surrounding countryside is parched, but from Labuhan
Pandan, 10km to the north, snorkeling and fishing trips to
offshore islands can be arranged.

LEMBAR   ✪

This is the ferry port for Bali but visitors who are whisked
away on buses to Senggigi or elsewhere miss little.
The nearby southwest peninsula is undeveloped but worth
exploring with your own
transport, preferably a
jeep. The road through the
peninsula runs through
Sekotong and Pelangan
before coming to an end
at Bangko Bangko, but
along the way there are
fishing villages where
boats can be chartered for
visits to small offshore
islands. This is relatively
unexplored territory and
visitors need their own
provisions.

Did you know ?

*Alfred Russel Wallace (1823–1913) proposed
the idea of an evolutionary distinction between Asia
and Australia. His division – later named
the Wallace Line – occurred between Bali and
Lombok because he believed that the immense depth
of the water (1,300m) prevented species from
migrating even when ocean levels fell during the
Ice Ages. Today, however, scientists believe the
differences in flora and fauna are accounted for
by different climatic conditions.*

A Walk on Gili Trawangan

Gili Trawangan (► 21) lies off the northwest coast of Lombok and a boat trip to the island takes only about 30 minutes.

This is a circular walk around the island, beginning at the point where you land after getting your feet wet disembarking. Turn to your left and head south, following the shore.

You will pass various stalls hiring out snorkeling gear and, on your right, a small shopping complex next to the popular Restoran Borobudur. Another 1km of walking takes you past the heart of the island's accommodation and there are numerous opportunities to stop and rest for a drink at any of the small restaurants.

The buildings gradually thin out as the southern end of the island is reached and the Sunset restaurant is one of the last places to be passed. On your right, the island's hill (100m) can be climbed as an excursion by taking one of the inland trails, and there are impressive views of Gunung Rinjani (► 83) and Gunung Agung (► 17) from the top. This hilltop is a popular place for watching the ocean sunset.

The path that runs along the west side of the island is devoid of buildings. The soil is thin and little can be seen growing apart from coconut trees, cacti and the occasional spread of eucalyptus. A small number of belled cattle and the odd goat may be encountered but that is likely to be all. As the path reaches the north of the island a trail heads inland passing a lighthouse beacon, but carry straight on. Shortly you will find tourist bungalows and restaurants reappearing.

From this point it is less than 1km to the disembarkation point where the walk began.

Boats depart regularly from Bangsal and Senggigi to the unspoiled Gili Islands

Distance
5km

Time
2 hours

Start/end point
Harbor (on eastern side of the island)
➕ 80A2

Lunch
Restoran Borobudur ($)
(► 99)

🕇 80B2
✉ 15km east of Ampenan
🕐 Pura Lingsar: open 24 hours daily
🚌 *Bemo* to Narmada from Sweta, then change for Lingsar
🖐 Pura Lingsar: cheap
↔ Narmada (▶ below)

A floral offering on the head of a demon-guard in Pura Lingsar

---

🕇 80B2
✉ 45km east of Ampenan
🚌 There is no regular *bemo* service to Loyok. Use your own transport
↔ Tetebatu (▶ 90)

🕇 80B2
✉ 10km east of Ampenan
🕐 Narmada Park: open daily 6–6
🚌 *Bemos* from Sweta
🖐 Narmuda Park: cheap
↔ Lingsar (▶ above), Suranadi (▶ 90)

LINGSAR ✪

The Wetu Telu temple, which is also known as Pura Lingsar, is the main attraction in Lingsar. It was constructed in 1714, rebuilt in 1878, and is unusual for its mixture of Hindu and Muslim Sasak devotees. The two religions have their own compounds, on different levels,

and the Sasak worshippers are members of a minority Muslim sect, the Wetu Telu. The higher courtyard is the Hindu place of worship while the lower one with its own pond is the Wetu Telu area. The pond is alive with eels, which devotees come to feed with hard-boiled eggs. Usually there are guides waiting outside to show you around but their knowledge may be limited.

LOYOK ✪

This little village's shops are noted for bamboo handicrafts. The bamboo table lamps and wall lamps are some of the better items on sale, but it is worth looking into more than one shop before making a purchase. The nearby village of Kotoraja (Town of Kings), 5km to the north on the road to Tetebatu, has a smaller selection of shops but is more notable for its blacksmithing tradition. Kotoraja was once a place of refuge for Lombok's rulers, hence its name.

NARMADA ✪✪

Taman Narmada (Narmada Park) was built in 1805 for King Anak Gede Karangasem of Mataram. It is claimed that the gardens, named after a sacred river in India, were designed to model Gunung Rinjani because the king was too frail to climb the real mountain. Apart from the main pond, supposed to model Rinjani's crater lake, Segara Anak (▶ 83), there is a pool open to the public for swimming. At weekends and holidays the park tends to fill up with daytrippers from the capital but when empty it is a pleasant spot to rest and relax in. There is a Balinese temple, Pura Kalasa, in the grounds and the remains of an aqueduct constructed by the Dutch next to the lake, a reminder of Lombok's colonial past.

The garden of Narmada (right) deserves more time than most organized trips allow

PRAYA ⊘⊘

The busy town of Praya is the hub for a number of craft villages in the surrounding area. Some 4km to the west is Sukarara village, noted for the quality of its weaving and a favorite stop with tour buses. Most of Sukarara's shops (▶108) have large displays, some have their own workshops, and material can be purchased by the meter. The village of Penujak, 6km to the southwest of Praya on the road to Kuta, is noted for its pottery (▶106) and watching the potters at work is one of the attractions. The finished products come in all shapes and sizes; unfortunately, a lot of it presents a luggage problem.

➕ 80B1
✉ 25km southeast of Ampenan
🚌 *Bemos* travel between Sweta and Praya

PURA BATU BOLONG ⊘

This Balinese temple in the Senggigi area is positioned on a rocky promontory. A natural hole in this rock accounts for the name Batu Bolong (Hollow Rock). Architecturally, the temple is unimpressive but there are excellent views across the Lombok Strait and visitors like to arrive in the evening to watch the sun setting over Bali.

➕ 80A2
✉ 2km south of Senggigi
🕐 24 hours daily
✋ Free
↔ Senggigi (▶25)

SADE ⊘⊘

This traditional Sasak village is well prepared for tourists and there is no escaping the company of a self-appointed young guide. Obligatory sights are the rice store, where only women are allowed to enter, and the clay made with the help of buffalo dung that keeps mosquitoes at bay. Sade is a tourist trap but, being on the main road, it is an easy stop for tour buses heading to Kuta. The village has no admission charge, but a small donation is expected when signing the visitors' book. Rembitan village, a little to the north, is much the same but does have an old mosque, closed on Mondays.

➕ 80B1
✉ 3km north of Kuta
🕐 Visit 8–6
🍴 Closest restaurants are in Kuta ($)
🚌 *Bemos* from Praya to Kuta (some direct from Sweta) stop at Sade
💰 Cheap
↔ Kuta (▶84)

SEGENTER

Beyond Bangsal, the coastal road that follows the shoreline around the north of Lombok is not often traveled by visitors, other than to reach Senaru for an ascent of Gunung Rinjani. Yet the traditional village of Segenter is worth a visit and is far less of a tourist trap than Sade in the south (▶ 87). There is no admission charge but visitors are expected to make a small donation when signing the visitors' book.

SENARU

Senaru is usually only visited by those setting off for a climb up Gunung Rinjani, but this small Sasak village has intrinsic interest. The villagers' lifestyle has been little affected by tourism and any opportunity to watch the farmers at work in their fields is rewarding. There is no admission charge but a donation is expected when you are asked to sign the visitors' book.

SENGGIGI (▶ 25, TOP TEN)

SESAOT

This little village is easily reached from Suranadi if you have your own transport. The journey is a rewarding one, traveling past villagers washing clothes in the river and with great views of Gunung Rinjani ahead of you. At the village a rickety bridge, barely navigable by car, leads into a forest with pleasant swimming and picnic spots. A 3km stroll further up the road leads to a smaller village which is also beside the river. Bring your own food and drinks for a picnic.

The white-sand beach at Sira has a remarkable pristine beauty

SIRA

This is one of those places that will be unrecognizable in ten years. This tiny village boasts one of the most beautiful beaches in Lombok, a glorious stretch of unbroken white sand looking across to the Gili Islands. Plans are afoot to build hotels and develop a tourist infrastructure but for now there is nothing here but sea, sand and palm trees.

A Drive into the Heart of Lombok

The drive begins in the Ampenan-Mataram-Cakranegara-Sweta conurbation.

The bus and *bemo* terminal in Sweta makes a useful starting point, as it is located on the main road that heads east.

Head east on the road signposted for Narmada (6km).

The park at Narmada (► 86) makes a pleasant first stop but consider a short diversion (7km) to Suranadi (► 90) for refreshments at the Suranadi Hotel. The signposted road to Suranadi is a left turn at Narmada.

From Narmada, continue east on the main road for 25km and take a poorly signposted (white on a blue background) turning on the left for Tetebatu.

This road first passes the craft villages of Loyok (► 86) and Kotaraja before heading north for Tetebatu (► 90). There are a number of tourist restaurants either side of the road approaching Tetebatu as well as one in the village itself.

From Tetebatu, return to the main road (11km) that links the east and west of Lombok and turn right (west). You can either return to Sweta or retrace part of the journey as far as the village of Kopang (9km) and turn left to Praya.

From Praya (► 87) the pottery village of Penujak and the weaving village of Sukarara may be visited.

Finally, return to Praya and turn left for Mataram.

After 19km the village of Kediri is reached and, if time allows, a diversion could be made from here to Gunung Pengsong (► 83) on the west coast.

Otherwise, follow the signs for the main road back to Mataram and Sweta where the journey began.

Distance
83km (excluding diversions to Suranadi or Praya)

Time
6–8 hours

Start/end point
Sweta
➕ 80B2

Lunch
Soedjono Hotel ($) (► 99)
✉ Tetebatu
☎ 0370-22159

SURANADI ✪✪

🕂 80B2
✉ 7km north of Narmada
🍴 Set meals ($$) and à la carte ($) in the Suranadi Hotel
🎫 Temple: free
↔ Narmada (► 86), Sesaot (► 88)

The holy temple of Suranadi is positioned close to a number of springs, which helps explain why it is named after a heavenly river in Hindu cosmology. The temple itself is unremarkable but the surroundings are pleasant. The nearby Suranadi Hotel was built by the colonial Dutch administration and, although it is architecturally dull, it nevertheless evokes a sense of the past; a bonus is its spring-water swimming pool which is open to non-residents for a small charge.

TETEBATU ✪✪

🕂 80B2
✉ 11km north of the main east–west road
🍴 Various places ($) before reaching the Soedjono Hotel

Tetebatu is a small village on the slopes of Gunung Rinjani. Lacking an obvious focus, such as a temple, it is the scenic and unspoilt countryside that creates Tetebatu's appeal. It is not a place to just visit and leave within an hour; the pleasure comes from strolling through the maze of trails that link the paddy fields. The splendid Jukut waterfall is a 6km walk to the east but shorter walks are also possible. Alternatively you can hire a guide and embark upon a longer excursion. As with other places in Lombok, the signs of a future tourist industry are plain to see, but for the moment this is still virgin territory. There is a reasonable choice of restaurants; the dining room of the colonial Soedjono Hotel has picturesque views. This is the best place in Lombok to buy fabrics.

Sasak children at Tetebatu gladly help their parents at harvest time

Where To...

Above: *paintings in the Kerta Gosa, Klungkung*
Right: *musicians and artists are everywhere in Bali*

South & Southeast Bali

Prices

Prices are graded into three categories:

$ = cheap
$$ = moderate
$$$ = expensive

Bukit Peninsula

The Ocean ($$$)

On the center of the Bukit peninsula's southern coast, perched on the side of a cliff 15m above the Indian Ocean. Tables for two under the moonlight with a sea breeze.

✉ **Bali Cliff Hotel, Ungasan**
☎ **0361-771992** ⏰ **11–10:30**

Candi Dasa

Kububali ($$$)

One of the smartest places to eat in Candi Dasa. An open kitchen, mostly seafood, and the best drinks menu in town.

✉ **The main street in town**
☎ **0363-41532** ⏰ **8–10**

Taj Mahal/Hawaii ($$)

A restaurant with a split personality? Suitably eclectic menu of Indian, European and Chinese dishes.

✉ **The main street in town**
☎ **0363-41138** ⏰ **9–10**

TJ's ($$)

Part of the very small Watergarden Hotel, this classy restaurant serves great Mexican food in an idyllic setting.

✉ **Next to the Watergarden Hotel on the main street**
☎ **0363-41540** ⏰ **9–10**

Denpasar

Puri Agung ($$)

European and Indonesian food best enjoyed amid the faded splendor of the hotel's main restaurant. Alternatively, there is also a poolside eating area.

✉ **Natour Bali Hotel, Jalan Veteran** ☎ **0361-225681**
⏰ **24 hours**

Kuta

Aromas Café ($$)

The best vegetarian restaurant, with blackboard specials and à la carte. Irresistible desserts. Try for a table at the back as the front area is brightly lit.

✉ **340 Jalan Legian**
☎ **0361-751003** ⏰ **8–11**

Bali Asi ($)

Just past TJs restaurant, this is a good-value, informal eatery popular with Australians. A huge menu, and pizza specials between noon and 5PM.

✉ **Poppies 1** ⏰ **7:30–10**

Bali Aussie Bar & Restaurant ($$)

No mistaking the clientele of this popular little roadside restaurant where the atmosphere is more important than the food.

✉ **69 Jalan Melasti**
☎ **0361-751910** ⏰ **8–11**

Bali Fish & Chips ($)

Very good Western-style fish and chips. Small eat-in area, but mainly for takeaways. Salt and vinegar on the tables!

✉ **Jalan Poppies II** ☎ **0361-750677** ⏰ **11–11**

Golden Lotus ($$–$$$)

Perhaps the best Chinese cuisine in Bali; the Szechuan dishes will not disappoint.

✉ **Bali Dynasty Hotel**
☎ **0361-752403** ⏰ **12–2, 6–10**

Hard Rock Café ($$$)

Serving top-quality burgers, steaks and other US-style fare, with music memorabilia as the surrounds.

Jalan Pantai, Kuta
☎ 0361-755661 🕐 11–2

Mandarin Restaurant ($$)
Cantonese, Szechuan and seafood served for lunch and dinner. Live music in the evening.
✉ Jalan Kartika Plaza, Tuban
☎ 0361-751369 🕐 11–3, 6–11

Maccaroni Club ($$)
The hip hang-out on the strip, with stylish decor and an excellent Italian/European menu.
✉ Jalan Legian ☎ 0361-754662 🕐 8–1AM

Mini Restaurant ($)
A large restaurant that might be better named the Maxi – or perhaps the name refers to the prices. Good-value seafood meals.
✉ 36 Jalan Legian ☎ 0361-751651 🕐 9–11

Poppies ($$)
A pleasant garden setting of pools and waterfalls surrounded by flowers. Make a reservation in advance because this place is very popular. Seafood, regional and Western dishes.
✉ Poppies 1 ☎ 0361-751059
🕐 8–11

TJs ($$)
This haven of tranquillity is tucked away down a lane running off the southern end of Jalan Legian. Mexican food.
✉ Poppies 1 ☎ 0361-751093
🕐 8:30–11

Warung Made ($$)
A smaller version of the sister restaurant in Seminyak, but this one is the original. Still a top venue for both local and international cuisine. A quiet and most welcome resting place from Kuta's madness.
✉ Jalan Pantai ☎ 0361-751923 🕐 8–12

Legian-Seminyak

Body & Soul ($$)
Funky deli-style eatery with home-baked breads and lots of eastern European flavors. Create your own anti pasto from a great array.
✉ Jalan Raya, Seminyak
☎ 0361-732769
🕐 8–12AM

Kura Kura ($$$)
Gourmet dining in this prestigious restaurant at The Oberoi. Specialties include grilled snapper, charcoal-grilled tuna steak and lobster.
✉ The Oberoi, Legian Beach
☎ 0361-730361 🕐 7–9.30

Ryoshi ($$)
Best sushi this side of Tokyo. A full Japanese menu with daily specials make this place a must for food lovers.
✉ Jalan Raya Seminyak,
☎ 0361-731152 🕐 12–12AM

Teras ($$)
Great open-air, roof-top venue for home-made pasta and oven-baked pizza. Lively evening atmosphere; busy at weekends.
✉ Jalan Raya, Seminyak
☎ 0361-730492 🕐 5–12AM

Yanies ($$)
Well-established restaurant and bar specializing in steaks and hamburgers, but with plenty of other choices.
✉ Jalan Tunjung Mekar, Legian ☎ 0361-751292
🕐 11–2AM

Nusa Dua

Brasserie des Celebrites ($$$)
Informal dining, reserve a table with a garden or sea view. This is a new restaurant, promising both 'bush tucker' and health-conscious food.
✉ Hotel Nikko Bali ☎ 0361-773377 🕐 6–11

Rijsttafel
One of many masterpieces in Indonesian cuisine is the *rijsttafel* (from the Dutch, meaning 'rice table'). The food was originally prepared by different households to feed returning soldiers, and it should consist of at least ten dishes, usually including shrimp crackers, hot chilli *sambal* paste, bean curd, spicy beef, chicken and duck – all served with yellow rice flavored with coconut milk. Delicious!

Balinese Desserts
Western desserts are often disappointing, so try some of the Indonesian ones made from sticky or glutinous rice, like *ketan* (sugary rice pudding with coconut milk) or *lemper* (fruit pudding, with the emphasis on pudding). Look out too for durian-flavoured ice cream and luridly colored sweets made from cassava.

Lagoona ($$$)
Seafood and continental dishes, theme nights, strolling musicians. Try local seafood like *bawal* or *baronang*.
✉ Bali Hilton Hotel
☎ 0361-771102 🕐 7–10.30

Hamabe ($$$)
Authentic Japanese cuisine, in an elegant environment overlooking a Japanese garden. *Shabu-shabu, teppanyaki, sukiyaki* and à la carte.
✉ Sheraton Nusa Indah Hotel
☎ 0361-771906 🕐 6–11

Makuwa Pakuwa ($$)
An open-air seafood restaurant in the Galleria complex. Free shuttle service.
✉ Galleria Nusa Dua Shopping Complex ☎ 0361-772252
🕐 11:30–11

Poco Loco ($$)
Mexican food with live music and a good drinks list. Free transport within Nusa Dua.
✉ Jalan Pantai Mengiat
☎ 0361-773923 🕐 6–12AM

Sateria ($$–$$$)
Salads, steaks, pizzas, grills. Beachside location, ideal for lunch or dinner. Mostly seafood in the evening, sometimes theme nights.
✉ Melici Bali Hotel
☎ 0361-771510 🕐 10–11

The Terrace and The Restaurant ($$$)
Two restaurants at the Amanusa hotel offering Bali's best in sophisticated fine dining. The Terrace overlooks a golf course and features European, Thai and Indonesian specialties. The Restaurant has the better wine list.
✉ Amanusa ☎ 0361-772333
🕐 11–2, 6–10

Sanur

Agung Bar & Restaurant ($$)
Small but tasty selection of European and local dishes, plus cocktails. Music on Tuesday and Friday. Close to Bali Hyatt hotel.
✉ 97 Jalan Danau Tamblingan
☎ 0361-288029 🕐 8–10

Koki Restaurant ($$)
Pub atmosphere with pool table and bar. Very popular with local Brits for its real pub grub: pies, bangers and mash – the real McCoy.
✉ Jalan Bypass Ngurah Rai
☎ 0361-287503 🕐 4–12

La Taverna ($$)
Beachside restaurant with excellent pizzas cooked over a wood fire. Indonesian favorites also available.
✉ La Taverna Bali Hotel, Jalan Danau Tamblingan
☎ 0361-288497 🕐 7–11

Laba-Laba ($)
Large menu, cosy during the evening, floor show on Monday and Friday.
✉ 134 Jalan Danau Tamblingan ☎ 0361-288132
🕐 8–9

Sita ($$)
Seafood and Indonesian food, nightly performances of traditional dances. Too touristy for some, so come with the right attitude. Free transport.
✉ Jalan Ngurah Rai/By Pass No 41 ☎ 0361-288468 🕐 7–10

Swastika Garden ($$)
Attractive garden setting with choice of Indonesian, Chinese, seafood and pasta. Traditional dances on Thursday and Sunday.
✉ Jalan Danau Tamblingan
☎ 0361-288573 🕐 6–10

Telaga Naga ($$$)
Across the road from the Bali Hyatt, this upmarket Chinese restaurant serves spicy Szechuan favourites and stir-fried Cantonese dishes. Thatched-grass roof surrounded by lotus ponds.
✉ Jalan Danau Tamblingan
☎ 0361-288271 🕐 6:30–10

Central & West Bali

Ubud Area

Ary's Warung ($$)

International and oriental food served in a relaxed setting with live music. The food is very good and the atmosphere aims to be cultured. Come here for the whole evening.

✉ Jalan Raya ☎ 0361-975053 🕐 9–1AM

Bumbu ($$)

Balinese, Indian, and vegetarian food in the heart of Ubud, opposite Puri Saren Agung (► 55).

✉ 1 Jalan Sueta ☎ 0361-974217 🕐 8:30–10

Café Lotus ($$)

Quality Asian food, as well as pasta dishes, served at this famous Ubud restaurant, named after the large lotus pond that it overlooks.

✉ Jalan Raya ☎ 0361-975660 🕐 8–10

Café Wayan ($$)

One of the best restaurants in Bali (see sidepanel), with a dining area stretching back in a series of thatched platforms. Indonesian, seafood, pizza, pasta and vegetarian dishes. Special dishes each night and on Sunday there is an evening buffet of regional dishes. Try the 'death by chocolate' dessert. Reservations necessary.

✉ Monkey Forest Rd ☎ 0361-975447 🕐 8–11

Cahaya Dewata Restaurant ($$$)

Transport needed to get here from central Ubud. Reserve a window table overlooking the gorge; there are great views at lunchtime, river sounds and twinkling lights of Denpasar at night. Indonesian, Japanese and European dishes. Salads and guacamole for appetizers.

✉ Cahaya Dewata Hotel, Kedewatan ☎ 0361-975495 🕐 7:30–10

Casa Luna ($$)

Wholesome Balinese food and some steaks, salads, excellent bread and vegetarian choices. Recommended for breakfast, lunch or dinner. Try for a table at the back for a river view. The restaurant runs Balinese cooking courses.

✉ Jalan Raya ☎ 0361-973283 🕐 8–10

The Chedi ($$$)

This lavish hotel restaurant serves great Indonesian and Western cuisine, overlooking a steep river valley.

✉ Payangan, Ubud ☎ 0361-975963 🕐 7–11. Closed Mon

Hotel Tjampuhan Restaurant ($$)

Arrive before dark and take a stroll around the beautiful grounds before retiring to the restaurant. Regional and international food served in this famous old hotel.

✉ Jalan Raya Campuhan, Hotel Tjampuhan ☎ 0361-975368 🕐 8–10

Ibu Rai ($)

Centrally located for people-watching on the street. Balinese dishes, spaghetti, seafood, wine.

✉ 72 Monkey Forest Rd ☎ 0361-975066 🕐 9–10

The Best Restaurant?

The Café Wayan restaurant was started in 1977 when Wayan Kelepon opened her own *warung* (inexpensive roadside restaurant or street stall). She sold rice to fellow Ubud residents, and soft drinks to tourists. Ten years later she opened Café Wayan with four tables. Now there are 45 tables and that's not enough to satisfy the demand. It is probably the best restaurant in Ubud and one of the best in all of Bali.

Ubud is Best
Ubud offers better value in quality dining than anywhere else in Bali or Lombok. Not even the sumptuous restaurants that adorn the top-class hotels of Nusa Dua can provide an equally accomplished range of international and local dishes and serve them in an appropriate atmosphere of artistic aplomb.

Kokokan Club ($$)
Delicious Thai food served in this well-established hotel restaurant that manages to create a refined atmosphere without pretensions or high prices.
✉ Jalan Pengosekan, Puri Indah Hotel ☎ 0361-975742 🕐 11–10

Kopi Bali ($)
Unassuming café with a happy hour (6–8) and a wide choice of regional dishes, steaks and seafood.
✉ Monkey Forest Road ☎ 0361-974226 🕐 9–11

Mumbul's ($)
Serves great pasta dishes as well as tasty Indonesian fare. Very suitable for vegetarians.
✉ Jalan Raya ☎ 0361-975364 🕐 11–10

Murni's Warung ($$)
Two levels with tables overlooking a river and tropical greenery. Mediterranean and Indonesian food, and curries. Give a day's notice for a Balinese feast of smoked duck.
✉ Jalan Raya, Campuhan ☎ 0361-975233 🕐 8:30–10

Nomad Bar & Restaurant ($)
Appetizers and main courses of fish, chicken, steaks and local dishes, such as pepesikan (grilled fish with herbs wrapped in a banana leaf with salad and rice).
✉ Jalan Raya (opposite the playing field) ☎ 0361-975114 🕐 9–11

Parkit Restaurant ($$)
A hotel restaurant serving Balinese and international food. Free transportation available in Central Ubud.
✉ Heritage Champlung Sari Hotel, Monkey Forest Road ☎ 0361-975418 🕐 8–10

Pita Maha Terrace Restaurant ($$–$$$)
Alfresco dining in a beautiful setting overlooking the valley of the Wos river. International and traditional specialities; a day's notice is needed for the roasted duck.
✉ Jalan Sanggingan,, Pita Maha Hotel ☎ 0361-974330 🕐 10–10

Puri's Bar & Restaurant ($)
An unpretentious place on the main road. There is noise from traffic sometimes, but this place is a handy antidote to shopping fatigue and close to Puri Saren Agung (► 55) for evening dances. Light meals as well as meat and vegetable dishes. Good value drinks.
✉ Jalan Raya 🕐 8–10 ☎ 0361-975608

Purimuwa ($)
Menus in English and German explain the Balinese dishes in detail. Try for a table at the back in the garden.
✉ Monkey Forest Rd ☎ 0361-975441 🕐 8–10

Ryoshi ($$)
Japanese restaurant, serving traditional sushi and tempura dishes. The fresh noodle dishes are exceptional and the sake is good on those cooler Ubud nights.
✉ Jalan Raya ☎ 0361-976362 🕐 12–12

North & East Bali

When it comes to the Lake Batur area there tends to be an inverse relationship between the quality of the food and the popularity of the destination. The sheer number of coach tours that disgorge hungry sightseers every lunchtime has led to a surfeit of plush and overpriced restaurants offering pre-cooked buffet lunches. With your own transport it is possible to escape by driving north from Penelokan towards Kintamani and looking for somewhere like Puncak Sari (► 58) where the food will not be wonderfully different but where there is more space and fewer people. Another possibility is the road in Toya Bungkah where there are a number of inexpensive and reasonably priced restaurants offering better food than anywhere in Penelokan itself.

In the north of Bali the best place to eat is undoubtedly Lovina. There are countless places to choose from on either side of the road and, tucked away down the side streets leading to the beach, there are plenty of inexpensive restaurants belonging to the homestays. There is healthy competition between the various establishments in Lovina and you can wander from one place to another checking menus and comparing prices. The actual differences in the cost of a meal need only concern those on a very tight budget; the availability of particular types of fresh fish is a more important consideration.

Singaraja may be the second largest city in Bali but from the visitor's point of view this is not reflected in the restaurant scene. The only place where a cluster of restaurants may be found is around a small square off Jalan Jen Achmad Yani near the corner with Jalan Pramuka. One of the best restaurants here is Gandi (► 98) but there are other places worth considering in this centrally located square.

Lovina

Aryas Cafe ($)

The Aryas café is a modest establishment with local dishes and some vegetarian choices, good desserts.

✉ Kalibukbuk ☎ 0362-41797
🕐 8:30–11

Astina ($)

Just 500m off the main road, within spitting distance of the beach, this restaurant serves inexpensive and simple food in modest surroundings.

✉ Kalibukbuk ☎ 0362-41187
🕐 7:30–10

Las Palmas ($–$$)

Pleasant beach-side hotel restaurant with Indian, Chinese and European food. Set in its own grounds with lush gardens.

✉ Palma Beach Hotel
☎ 0362-41775 🕐 7–10

Lian Seafood Restaurant ($$)

Opposite the Aditya bungalows and not on the beach side of road, but the seafood (squid, crab, lobster and prawn) is very good. Local wine available. Husband in the kitchen, wife serving.

✉ Kaliasem, just west of Kalibukbuk ☎ 0362-41480
🕐 10–11

A *Warung*

Warung has no exact translation – food stall, transport café, take-out. It may be a rough shed with a few tables or perhaps on wheels at the side of the pavement. A *warung* often offers the best way to taste Indonesian food – the ingredients are always fresh and competition stiff, so owners really pride themselves on offering their best home cooking. The simple rule of thumb – always eat at the busiest stall. A night market can be the best place to be adventurous and try some of the pure Indonesian food they offer; just point to something that looks interesting – *cap cai* (cooked vegetables) or *nasi goreng* (fried rice).

Lovina

The restaurant scene in the north of Bali is to be found in the beach-resort area of Lovina, 10km west of Singaraja. Lovina stretches for over 8km but most places to eat are clustered either side of the village of Kalibukbuk, which is situated on the main road. Here you will find more than a dozen restaurants, many of them specializing in fish dishes and all of them offering good value for money.

Malibu ($)

One of the liveliest restaurants in Lovina with live music from 10PM to 1AM. Telephone to ask about free transport. The food is not wonderful but there is a great choice and the drinks list is very satisfying. Good for breakfast also.

✉ Kalibukbuk ☎ 0362-41671 🕙 8–1

Mandhara Chico ($)

This hotel and restaurant is at the eastern end of Lovina, opposite the petrol station. The restaurant is a cut above the usual budget places dotted between here and Kalibukbuk. Tourist fare.

✉ Anturan, 5km east of Kalibukbuk ☎ 0362-41476 🕙 7:30–10

Puri-Bali ($)

The restaurant belonging to Puri-Bali Bungalows is very close to the beach and mostly serves seafood and steaks. Relaxing and informal.

✉ Kalibukbuk ☎ 0362-41485 🕙 7:30–10

Tanjung Alam ($)

You can't get any closer to the beach than this – waves almost lap over the tables! Come here for an evening meal and watch the sun set. Seafood and Western dishes.

✉ Kaliasem, just west of Kalibukbuk ☎ 0362-41223 🕙 10–10

Penelokan

Puncak Sari ($)

Penelokan is not short of restaurants offering lunch buffets but one large coach party can take them over. This restaurant is outside the center so there is less risk of congestion and the view from the outside tables is spectacular.

✉ 2km north of Penelokan on road to Kintamani ☎ 0366-51073 🕙 10–4

Singaraja

Gandi ($)

An unpretentious restaurant just off the main street away from the traffic. Mostly Indonesian and Chinese dishes with vegetarian choices. Its popularity with the locals is the best recommendation.

✉ 25 Jalan Jen Achmad Yani ☎ 0362-21163 🕙 8–8

Tirtagangga

Tirta Ayu ($)

It is worth timing your visit to the Water Palace in Tirtagangga (► 22) so that you can enjoy a meal at the Tirta Ayu restaurant inside its grounds. The food is not especially good, but the delightful setting overlooking the pools and greenery makes this the best place for a meal in this corner of Bali.

✉ Water Palace ☎ 0363-21697 🕙 7–6

Toya Bungkah (Lake Batur)

Under the Volcano ($)

There are two restaurants and hotels with this name, just a few hundred meters apart, situated close to the shore of Lake Batur. Under the same management, the restaurants offer better food than most of the local competition. Regional and Western dishes.

✉ Toya Bungkah 🕙 7–10

Lombok

Gili Trawangan

Restoran Borobudur ($)
Centrally located next to the main cluster of shops. Very popular, seafood, steak, Indonesian dishes.
✉ **Near where boats dock**
🕐 7:30–10

Sunset ($)
Located further south than the main concentration of restaurants, this restaurant is handy after climbing the nearby hill. Simple pasta and chicken dishes, sandwiches and omelets.
✉ **South end of island, facing the sea** 🕐 8–11

Kuta

Kuta Indah Hotel Restaurant ($$)
Within walking distance of a lovely beach. No surprises in the menu but, until the big new resorts take over, this is the best place for a meal in southern Lombok.
✉ **Kuta Indah Hotel, Kuta**
☎ 0370-654628 🕐 7–10

Senggigi

Blue Coral ($$)
Friendly, candlelit tables but informal, attached to diving school of same name on the main street. Meat, seafood and Japanese food (but skip the pizza).
✉ **Jalan Raya Senggigi**
☎ 0370-693002 🕐 8–11

Kafé Alberto ($$)
Located in the Art Market, serving pizzas, Indonesian food and barbecues. Touristy, but with superb sea views.
✉ **Jalan Raya Senggigi**
☎ 0370-693390 🕐 10–10

Kartika Senggigi ($)
Vast menu with some interesting specialties like sautéed tofu with local fish. Squid, lobster, prawn, crab and satay.
✉ **Jalan Raya Senggigi**
☎ 0370-693587 🕐 9–10:30

Kebun Rohani ($$)
Pleasing little restaurant, near the Sheraton, specializing in barbecued seafood.
✉ **Jalan Raya Senggigi**
☎ 0370-693018 🕐 7:30–10

Naga ($$)
Belonging to a split-site hotel, the Naga restaurant is on the inland side of the road opposite the beach-facing accommodation. Chinese, seafood and Thai food.
✉ **Jalan Raya Senggigi**
☎ 0370-693101 🕐 10–10

Princess of Lombok ($$)
Mexican favorites and steaks, poor choice of desserts. A pub downstairs with darts and billiards.
✉ **Jalan Raya Senggigi**
☎ 0370-693011 🕐 7:30–11

Sunshine Restaurant ($)
An informal Chinese seafood restaurant facing the sea. The day trips to Gili Trawangan depart near by. Good value.
✉ **Jalan Raya Senggigi**
☎ 0370-693232 🕐 8–10

Tetebatu

Soedjono Hotel Restaurant ($)
The restaurant has fine views over the thatched roofs of the hotel bungalows to rice paddies beyond. Indonesian food.
✉ **Soedjono Hotel, Tetebatu**
☎ 0370-622159
🕐 6:30–11

The Rambutan
The rambutan is sometimes known as the hairy lychee (*rambut* is Indonesian for hair) because the two fruits taste almost alike. Don't be alarmed when confronted with the startlingly red (and very hairy) skin, simply peel it off and eat the pearl-white fruit within. Avoid the seed in its centre – it is said to be narcotic!

South & Southeast Bali

Prices
Prices are graded into three categories:

$ = cheap
$$ = moderate
$$$ = expensive

Candi Dasa

Amankila ($$$)
The Amankila hotel boasts 35 rooms starting at about US$400 a night, exclusively located on a beachfront plateau with spectacular views of the Indian Ocean. The tiered swimming pool is unique in Bali, the suites are luxurious.
✉ **Manggis (PO Box 133, Klungkung 80701)** ☎ **0363-41333**

Candi Dasa Ashram ($$)
This is an ashram (a place of religious retreat) and guests may participate in some of the meditation sessions, but there is no obligation. All meals are strictly vegetarian and are included in the room rate. The ashram has a splendid location close to the beach. No hot water.
✉ **Off Candi Dasa's main road, next to a lagoon** ☎ **0363-41108**

Ida Candi Dasa ($)
Bungalows with verandas, fans and cold water, looking out onto a pretty garden that reaches down to the sea. Breakfast served in the rooms. Ida Candi Dasa is one of the best budget places in Candi Dasa.
✉ **Entrance on Candi Dasa's main road** ☎ **No phone**

Kelapa Mas ($)
Kelapa Mas is located right on the beach with a traditional Balinese garden, friendly staff and a restaurant. There is hot water, but no air-conditioning. Suitable for families.
✉ **Candi Dasa Beach (PO Box 103, Amlapura 80801)** ☎ **0363-41947**

Kuta-Legian

Agung Cottages ($$)
In the very heart of Kuta. Most rooms have air-conditioning but less expensive rooms without air-conditioning (but with fans) are also available. You can't get more central than this.
✉ **Jalan Legian** ☎ **0361-757427**

Bali Garden ($$$)
Popular with Australians, within walking distance of Kuta's beach, shops, bars and restaurants.
✉ **Jalan Kartika (PO Box 1101)** ☎ **0361-752725**

Bali Indah ($)
Basic but very reasonably priced. A bed, shower and toilet.
✉ **Poppies Lane 11** ☎ **0361-752509**

Bali Padma ($$$)
Top-notch hotel in Legian, over 400 rooms, with one of the best tropical gardens of any hotel in Bali.
✉ **Corner of Jalan Pantai Kuta and Jalan Melasti** ☎ **0361-752111**

Karthi Inn ($$)
Three levels with all the rooms overlooking the swimming pool. Well located for shopping expeditions in Kuta.
✉ **Jalan Kartika Plaza** ☎ **0361-754810**

Marsa Inn ($–$$)
A haven of peace in the middle of Kuta, with a choice of rooms with or without air-conditioning.
✉ **Poppies Lane 1** ☎ **0361-758507**

Natour Kuta Beach ($$$)

The only hotel with direct access to the beach, an advantage of being built on the site of the first hotel in Kuta. The original hotel was begun by an American couple and prospered until World War II (➤ 38).

✉ **Jalan Pantai No 1 (PO Box 3393)** ☎ **0361-751361**

Okie House ($)

Tucked away down a lane off Jalan Legian, the Okie House is good budget accommodation. Clean rooms, hot water and a fan; breakfast included.

✉ **Poppies Lane 11, Jalan Legian** ☎ **0361-752081**

Poppies Cottages 1 ($$–$$$)

Despite being in the center of Kuta, this delightful hotel manages to maintain an air of calm. Thatched cottages set in lovely secluded gardens and there is a good swimming pool.

✉ **Poppies Lane 1** ☎ **0361-751059**

Nusa Dua

Amanusa ($$$)

Set apart – and not just physically – from the other Nusa Dua resort hotels. Like the other two Aman resorts in Bali, the architecture, decor and views are outstanding.

✉ **Nusa Dua** ☎ **0361-772333**

Bali Hilton ($$$)

At the southern end of the beach, with the full range of amenities and facilities. Good restaurants and reliable service.

✉ **PO Box 46, Nusa Dua** ☎ **0361-771102**

Melici Bali ($$$)

This Spanish-run hotel group has over 500 rooms here, set in 10ha of lush gardens. Good restaurants and sports facilities.

✉ **Kawasan Wisata BTDC Lot 1, Nusa Dua** ☎ **0361-771510**

Sheraton Laguna ($$$)

The ultimate swimming pool, complete with sandy beaches and waterfalls, with a hotel built around it. The best rooms have direct access to the pool. A real playground of a hotel.

✉ **PO Box 17, Nusa Dua Beach** ☎ **0361-771327**

Sanur

Bali Hyatt ($$$)

Occupying 14 hectares between the beach and the road. The tropical opulence of the gardens and architecture is impressive and there are five restaurants to choose from.

✉ **Jalan Danau Tamblingan** ☎ **0361-288271**

Hotel Sanur Aerowisata ($$$)

At the southern end of the beach, this huge hotel has all the luxuries necessary for a lazy beach holiday.

✉ **Jalan Danau Tamblingan** ☎ **0361-288011**

Tirtagangga

Tirta Ayu Homestay ($)

Situated inside the Water Palace, with one very good room with a fan and delightful private outdoor shower. Other rooms with plain indoor showers. The climate is cooler here.

✉ **Tirtagangga** ☎ **0363-21697**

The Best?

What is the best hotel in Bali? If your priority is a swimming pool then the Sheraton Lagoona (a pool with a hotel around the edges: ➤ this page) and Amankila (exquisite tiered pools and an olympic-sized one: ➤ 100) are close competitors. For Balinese ambience and luxury the Pita Maha in Ubud (➤ 102) is hard to beat. For a sense of history try the nearby Hotel Tjampuhan (➤ 102). For sheer class and sublimely good taste it is hard to beat any one of the three Aman hotels: Amankila (➤ 100), Amanusa (➤ this page), Amandari (➤ 102).

Central & West Bali

Hotels and *Losmen*

Accommodation places that call themselves hotels are usually the larger establishments where one can expect a swimming pool and air-conditioning in all the rooms. Smaller places are often called *losmen* or homestays because the proprietor usually lives close by and there is often a choice of rooms and cottages with or without air-conditioning.

Ubud Area

Amandari ($$$)

Another of the three Aman luxury hotels in Bali. The suites are elegantly beautiful, the atmosphere is one of sublime indulgence, and the views are fabulous.

✉ **Sayan/Kedewatan**
☎ **0361-975333**

Bali Spirit ($$$)

In a peaceful rural area outside Ubud in the valley of the Wos River with superb views. The traditional art and furnishings include imaginative touches to the rooms, like the bathrooms featuring inlaid stone. Spa services, massages, pool, beauty salon, and free transport around the Ubud area for shopping, dining and dance performances.

✉ **Nyuhkuning (PO Box 189, Ubud 80571)** ☎ **0361-974012**

Cahaya Dewata ($$$)

The deluxe rooms all overlook the River Ayung in the village of Kedewatan. The standard rooms have garden views. Smallish pool. It helps to have your own transport as it is too far to walk between the hotel and central Ubud and there are plenty of art galleries along the road.

✉ **Kedewatan** ☎ **0361-975495**

Gerebig Bungalows ($)

Excellent accommodation in the delightful village of Penestanan. Clean rooms with balconies overlooking rice fields, 30m off the main road through the village.

✉ **Penestanan (PO Box 212, Ubud)** ☎ **0361-974582**

Hotel Tjampuhan ($$$)

Cottage accommodation with verandas overlooking a picturesque valley, built around the home of artist Walter Spies, whose 1930s house is one of the more expensive rooms. The gardens are exquisite.

✉ **Jalan Raya Campuhan (PO Box 198, Ubud 80571)** ☎ **0361-975368**

Pertiwi Bungalows ($$)

Centrally located, halfway down Monkey Forest Road, with relaxing gardens, rooms with balconies and Balinese decor, and a medium-sized pool.

✉ **Monkey Forest Road**
☎ **0361-975236**

Pita Maha ($$$)

A luxury hotel with beautifully designed villas and tasteful Balinese decor. One of the most luxurious and elegant hotels in Bali. Free bus to and from town.

✉ **Jalan Sanggingan (PO Box 198, Ubud 80571)** ☎ **0361-974330**

Puri Bunga Village Hotel ($$$)

Picturesque location overlooking River Ayung. Small swimming pool but terrific views from the rooms. Transport needed to reach central Ubud.

✉ **Kedewatan** ☎ **0361-975488**

Wartini ($)

A good example of a typical Ubud homestay with a friendly atmosphere and good rooms. Tucked away down a side street off the main road through Peliatan.

✉ **Off Jalan Raya, Peliatan**
☎ **0361-973281**

North & East Bali & Lombok

North & East Bali

Lovina

Aditya Bungalows ($$)
Air-conditioned cottages with verandas. Good facilities include pool – all for far less than you'd pay in southern Bali.
✉ Kaliasem ☎ 0362-41059

Bali Lovina Beach Cottages ($$)
Balinese-style cottages on waterfront, with pool and poolside bar, air-conditioning.
✉ Pantai Lovina ☎ 0362-41285

Palma Beach Hotel ($$)
Close to a shallow stretch of beach safe for swimming and children. Facilities include pool.
✉ Jalan Raya ☎ 0362-41775

Rambutan Beach Cottages ($–$$)
Attractive beach-side cottages in a tropical garden with pool. Hot water available; no air-conditioning. Good restaurant.
✉ Kalibukbuk ☎ 0362-41388

Taman Lily's ($)
Six elegant cottages with verandas facing a small garden. Hot water, but no air–conditioning. By the beach.
✉ Kalibukbuk ☎ 0362-41307

Lombok

Kuta

Kuta Indah ($–$$)
Near the beach and hills, the first of many functional new hotels in this area of Lombok.
✉ Kuta ☎ 0370-654628

Novotel Lombok Coralia ($$)
Moderately priced resort with good facilities. Architecture reflects local Sasak style.
✉ Pantai Putri Nyale ☎ 0370-653333

Senggigi

Kebun Rohani ($)
Thatched bamboo cottages. Mosquito nets and a mattress, breakfast included.
✉ Jalan Senggigi ☎ 0370-693018

Graha Senggigi Beach Hotel ($$)
One of the best Senggigi resort hotels.
✉ Jalan Raya Senggigi ☎ 0370-693101

Lombok Intan Laguna ($$$)
Good facilities, including tennis, gym and sauna, swimming pool and a restaurant open 24 hours.
✉ Jalan Raya Senggigi ☎ 0370-693090

Pondok Shinta ($)
Very basic (bed, shower and small fan) and very inexpensive rooms. Easy access to the beach.
✉ Jalan Raya Senggigi ☎ 0370-693012

Sheraton Senggigi ($$$)
Perfect beach location with good shade and a pool that children will love.
✉ Jalan Raya Senggigi. ☎ 0370-693333

Suranadi

Suranadi Hotel
This former Dutch residence has pleasant grounds, tennis court and spring-fed pool.
✉ 7km north of Narmada ☎ 0370-633686

Tetebatu

Soedjono Hotel ($)
Built in the 1930s as a private home, frequented by the Dutch, and a hotel since 1983. Spring-water swimming pool.
✉ Tetebatu, Sikur ☎ 0370-622159

Accommodation in Lombok
Visitors staying in less expensive accommodation in Lombok will miss the decor and craftwork of Ubud homestays and their small touches such as the complimentary flask of tea. A lot of accommodation in Senggigi is in modern hotels with comfortable rooms and facilities such as swimming pools, and the rest of the island is developing along similar lines. The best place to find budget rooms is the Gili Islands.

Balinese Paintings

Paintings

The range and quality of paintings for sale in Ubud is astonishing and it pays to shop around before making a decision. If the painting is purchased in its frame there may be a problem fitting it in your luggage, so consider negotiating a price without a frame and ask the gallery to roll up the painting inside a cardboard tube.

Kuta

C-Line Restaurant Gallery
Good Indonesian contemporary paintings.
✉ Jalan Kartika Plaza
☎ 0361-751285

Ubud Area

Agung Rai
The Agung Rai gallery is probably the most famous and reputable place in Ubud. There are seven galleries in all here with high-quality paintings ranging in price from the affordable to the astronomical.
✉ Jalan Peliatan ☎ 0361-975449

Ibu Rai
Ibu Rai is an artist specializing in modern themes. Some negotiation over prices is possible.
✉ Jalan Monkey Forest
☎ 0361-975066

I Nyoman Jerit
One of the first galleries on the left upon entering Penestanan from Campuan, two shops away from the Sri Ratih cottages. The prices are not outrageous.
✉ Penestanan, Ubud

K Sudana
K Sudana is an artist who likes painting faces but there is other material on display.
✉ Jalan Raya Campuhan, just beyond the Pita Maha hotel
☎ 0361-975731

Komaneka
One of the more upmarket galleries in Ubud with an excellent range of quality paintings. Make sure you take a look at the visitors' book as it makes interesting reading.
✉ Jalan Monkey Forest
☎ 0361-976090

Rahmat Agung
A group of three painters display their work for sale here and it is worth a browse, although the quality varies. Bargain for around 40 percent off the first price quoted.
✉ Jalan Sanggingan

Sunari
The Sunari gallery is close to the Neka Museum, and sells a fair selection of different styles of painting.
✉ Jalan Raya Sanggingan
☎ 0361-975808

Wayan Wijaya
If you are in Campuan (▶ 54) this small studio is worth a visit. As well as the usual scenes of village life, there are interesting modern themes.
✉ Payogan, Ubud

Varia
There may be not be any masterpieces here but a reasonable selection includes whimsical frogs cavorting in a Balinese landscape and immense canvases of tropical plants. Expect a 40 percent discount.
✉ Jalan Sanggingan

Sanur

Wianta's
A good selection of genuine contemporary paintings.
✉ Jalan Pandu, 300 meters from the Renon junction on the road to Denpasar

Jewelry

Celuk

Dharma Putra Silver
In the middle of the village. A big selection but it helps to have some idea of prices before entering into negotiations here.
✉ Celuk ☎ 0361-298634

Indarti Silver
On the left shortly after entering the village from Ubud, the stock is mostly earrings.
✉ Celuk ☎ 0361-298172

Murti I
In the middle of the village, this shop has interesting designs. Expect a 50 percent discount.
✉ Celuk ☎ 0361-298018

Kuta

Jonathan Gallery
A reputable shop selling gold and silver jewelry. Fixed prices in US dollars.
✉ 109 Jalan Legian ☎ 0361-754209

Suarti
The imaginative window displays single out these jewelry shops. As well as the two outlets listed below, there are Suarti shops at the Mastapa Garden Hotel, Jalan Legian, Kuta (☎ 0361-751660), at 404 Jalan Legian, Legian (☎ 0361-756094) and on Jalan Monkey Forest, Ubud (☎ 0361-974194).
✉ Jalan Bakung Sari and Poppies Lane 11 ☎ 0361-754899

Yusuf's Silver
Another reputable shop along Jalan Legian. All the prices of rings, earrings and chains are fixed.
✉ 85 Jalan Legian ☎ 0361-752050

Ubud

Ayu Silver
Reasonably priced bangles, bracelets and rings. Bargaining required.
✉ Jalan Monkey Forest ☎ 0361-294810

Putra Silver
Three outlets in Ubud, all with fixed prices. Rings, earrings, bracelets and chains.
✉ Jalan Monkey Forest ☎ 0361-975178

Ubud Corner
The same merchandise tends to turn up again and again in many of the jewelry shops, but this shop has more original necklaces and earrings. Prices are fixed but ask for 10 percent discount if purchasing two or more items.
✉ Jalan Monkey Forest ☎ 0361-974009

Lombok

Senggigi
Apart from a small selection in Senggigi's Art Market and Pacific Supermarket (► 107), there is little in the way of jewelry for sale in Lombok. However, at the southern end of Senggigi's main street there are two or three very small shops, with no names even to their stores, selling bangles and necklaces made from bone and colored stones. The more interesting items come from other Indonesian islands to the east of Lombok.
✉ Jalan Raya Senggigi

Choose with Care
Celuk and Kuta are the two best places for buying jewelry and many people think that some of Kuta's shops are able to offer the more imaginative and original designs. In both places, though, look for sturdily made pieces and avoid those that look as if they could easily come apart (because they probably will!). The sturdiness of the product is as important a consideration as the price when purchasing jewelry in Bali.

Arts & Crafts

Negotiating Skills
Shopping in Bali or Lombok requires bargaining skills and many inexperienced visitors end up regretting the prices they paid for their early purchases. If time allows, delay a purchase until different prices have been compared for similar goods, and try to avoid making your offer (which you can never reduce) until the seller makes at least one reduction on their opening price.

Banjar Tega

Bali Spice
When visiting the hot springs west of Lovina at Banjar Tega (► 70) stock up on supplies of spices not so readily available back home – saffron, vanilla, tamarind and black chillies.
✉ **Outside the entrance to the hot springs**

Candi Dasa

Asri
Masks, woodcarvings, batik cloth, mirrors, decorated frames and so on. Fixed, reasonable prices. Open until 11PM.
✉ **Jalan Raya Candi Dasa**
☎ **0363-41098**

Denpasar

Arts of Asia
For genuine antiques. Behind Lokitasari shopping center.
✉ **Jalan Thamrin 27–37**
☎ **0361-423350**

Kuta

Golden Buffalo
It claims to have the biggest range of bronze products in all of Indonesia. There is also a branch on Monkey Forest Road in Ubud.
✉ **1A Jalan Padma Timur**
☎ **0361-755936**

Sedana Pertiwi
Chess sets, wind chimes, wooden flowers, decorations for the home and souvenirs.
✉ **Jalan Buni Sari** ☎ **0361-751758**

Shopping Complex
Entered opposite the Bali Garden Hotel and close to McDonald's, this pedestrian precinct has a number of upmarket jewelry and antique shops, boutiques and art-and-crafts places. All fixed-price.
✉ **Jalan Kartika Plaza**

Uma
The shop is virtually dedicated to candle stands. Also sells letter holders, frames and mirrors.
✉ **355 Jalan Legian** ☎ **0361-757743**

Mas

Adhi
One of the big arts-and-crafts shops in Mas. Hundreds of resplendent masks and wooden fruits, from single apples to an entire pineapple tree! Prices are marked but negotiable.
✉ **Main road through Mas, at the Ubud end** ☎ **0361-975228**

Pantheon Gallery
Approaching Mas from the south, this is one of the first mansion-like shops on the left. Expect 50 percent off the first price quoted for the Buddhas, statues and wall hangings but aim as high as a 70 percent discount.
✉ **Main road through Mas, southern end** ☎ **0361-975224**

Villa Interiors
Quality furniture, including bureaux and chairs, and smaller items for the home, such as stationery boxes. Shipping can be arranged.
✉ **Jalan Raya** ☎ **0361-974050**

Penujak, Lombok

Mandalika
One of the specialist shops in the pottery village of

Penujak in Lombok. Mostly pots in a wide variety of sizes but also some lamps, ashtrays and attractive plates with fish designs.

✉ **Jalan Selong Blanak**

Sanur

Art Market

Stalls selling a wide choice of arts and crafts: masks, woodcarvings, screen-printed fans, batik shirts and so on.

✉ **Northern end of Jalan Danau Tamblingan**

Asano Art & Craft

Expensive but exquisite sewing boxes are typical of the good quality products.

✉ **69 Jalan Danau Tamblingan**
☎ **0361-289441**

Senggigi, Lombok

Art Market

At this shopping complex, close to the Sheraton Hotel, you will find that bargaining is necessary.

✉ **Jalan Raya Senggigi**

Asmara Art Shop

One of the better art shops in Lombok, at the Sheraton Hotel end of the village. Baskets, cloth, pottery and wood carvings.

✉ **Jalan Raya Senggigi**
☎ **0370-693109**

Pacific Supermarket

The upper level of this huge supermarket, at the Sheraton Hotel end of the main road, is devoted to arts and crafts from all over Lombok. The quality is generally poor but it's a good place to get an idea of prices before going elsewhere.

✉ **Jalan Raya Senggigi**
☎ **0370-693005**

Tampaksiring

Mawar

Situated at the Ubud end of this long village, all the products are made from wood – decorative cats and dogs, fruit, coconut earrings and lots more. Inexpensive.

✉ **Tampaksiring** ☎ **0361-901256**

Ubud Area

The Duck Man of Bali

A famous store on the Ubud–Gianyar road, near Goa Gajah. The shop sells wooden ducks – hundreds of them in all sizes and colors. Prices reflect sizes. Cheaper quackers are upstairs.

✉ **Tengkulak Kaja, Jalan Goa Gajah** ☎ **0361-975305**

Made Budiasa

Wood carvings ranging in size from small dancing frogs to massive demons that need shipping home. Easily found on the main road from Ubud to Gianyar, just past the turning for Denpasar.

✉ **Jalan Goa Gajah** ☎ **0361-976082**

Rai Sandi

Close to the Pita Maha hotel, this shop specializes in colorful masks and mobiles of Balinese dancers.

✉ **Jalan Raya Campuhan**
☎ **0361-975119**

Wora Shop

Halfway down the road on the left from the Puri Saren Agung end, this shop specializes in *ikat* wall hangings and so-called antiques. Can be expensive.

✉ **Jalan Monkey Forest**
☎ **0361-975675**

Shipments Home

Serious shoppers face the problem of transporting home a purchase too big or heavy for the airplane. In Kuta there are agents specializing in shipping home purchases, but the better shops will be able to make the arrangements for you. Other considerations include insurance, import duties, and the fact that wood products may crack when exported to drier climates. Ceramics fired at low temperatures are particularly fragile.

Clothes

Ikat Cloth

Ikat is a traditional southeast Asian method of patterning cloth so that complex patterns of colors can be built up through the weaving process. Its most distinguishable characteristic is the fuzzy blurring of one color into another, caused by the different dyes bleeding into one another.

Kuta

Art Market

There are numerous stalls and small shops here with their wares flowing out onto the pavement, but there is no actual art to be found in this market. Instead you can browse through the colorfully patterned beach dresses and shorts, racks of baggy cotton pants and T-shirts.

✉ **End of Jalan Bakung Sari, near the beach**

Pusaka

This shop sells good-quality T-shirts with interesting designs. It also stocks batik cloth. Batik cloth has colorful designs produced by applying wax to the parts to be left untreated. Pusaka is located at the top end of Jalan Legian, not far from the vegetarian Aromas Café (➤ 92).

✉ **338 Jalan Legian**

Animale

One of the best clothes shops in Bali, especially for women – the men's section is mostly smart T-shirts and beach shorts. There is another branch in Ubud (➤ below).

✉ **Kuta Square, Jalan Pantai Kuta** ☎ **0361-752717**

Uluwatu

Dresses and blouses (and sheets and pillowcases) made from handmade Balinese lace. Good quality and should withstand repeated washings. There is also a branch in Galleria Nusa Dua (➤ 109).

✉ **Jalan Legian, near Poppies Lane** ☎ **0361 751933**

Sukarara, Lombok

Dharma Setya

Ikat cloth, priced according to quality (which varies from the mediocre to the outstanding). The workshop is in a separate building and is worth visiting to see how the cloth is woven.

✉ **Jalan Tenun** ☎ **0370-654870**

Ubud Area

Animale

This is one of the best clothes shops in Ubud and is a sister shop to Animale in Kuta (➤ above), with a similar selection of good quality women's clothes.

✉ **Jalan Raya, Ubud** ☎ **0361-978549**

Bagus

Bagus is one of the few clothes shops outside the Kuta area with a stock that goes beyond T-shirts, shorts, and cheap dresses that lose their color after a few washes. It has mostly rayon and cotton dresses, blouses and some matching sets. Sizes can be made to order in two days.

✉ **Jalan Dewi Sita** ☎ **0361-976611**

Jani's

A wide range of high quality *ikat* textiles from around the Indonesian archipelago.

✉ **Jalan Monkey Forest**

Wardhani's Shop

Clothing, hand-woven material and silk, all at reasonable prices. They also stock ready-made temple clothing.

✉ **Jalan Monkey Forest**

Miscellaneous

Candi Dasa

Candi Bookstore
The best selection of second-hand books outside of Kuta. English, German, French, Swedish, Dutch, Italian and other editions.
✉ 45 Jalan Raya Candi Dasa

Denpasar

Toko Bhinneka Jaya
Balinese coffee makes a great souvenir and this company is Bali's biggest producer and distributor.
✉ Jalan Gajah Mada 80
☎ 0361-222053

Kuta

Billabong
One of the many specialist surfers' shops in Kuta selling surfing gear and garments.
✉ 16 Jalan Buni Sari
☎ 0361-752541

Matahari Department Stores
Two department stores, selling clothes, jewelry, watches and much more. Fixed prices and air conditioning are the advantages of browsing through the Kuta Square branch. Open until 10:30PM.
✉ Legian Plaza, Jalan Legian; Kuta Square

Nusa Dua

Galleria
A little soulless but a very convenient shopping complex in Nusa Dua. Jewelers, a supermarket, sports wear, an optician and designer-wear boutiques. Free shuttle buses to and from all the Nusa Dua hotels.
✉ Nusa Dua ☎ 0361-771662

Galeri Keris
This department store has a full range of wood carvings and other art and crafts, as well as fabrics, perfume and clothes. Useful for establishing prices or for buying last-minute souvenirs and presents.
✉ Galleria ☎ 0361-771303

Sheraton Nusa Indah Shopping Arcade
The Sheraton Nusa Indah has a better selection of shops than the other hotels in Nusa Dua. Clothes, fashion accessories, crafts and jewelry make up the content of most of the upmarket shops.
✉ Sheraton Nusa Indah Hotel

Sanur

Bali Harum
A gift shop with above-average merchandise. There are also outlets in Jalan Legian Tengah in Legian and in Jalan Raya in Seminyak.
✉ Jalan Danau Tamblingan
☎ 0361-286475

Ubud Area

Ganesha Bookshop
Stocks a wide variety of new books in English, including Bali guides, literature classics and highbrow Indonesian cultural and anthropological studies. An assortment of modern fiction is available secondhand as well as ethnic music CDs and tapes. Check out some of the local musical instruments, like flutes and drums (all for sale) and the unusual souvenirs and gifts.
✉ Jalan Raya, Ubud ☎ 0361-973359

Fixed Prices
Shopping for souvenirs and gifts can prove a time-consuming process. Comparing prices, negotiating in one shop and then another shop all takes time. The department stores in Kuta and Nusa Dua have fixed prices and you can browse without the sales chat. What you may lose by way of the price you may consider worthwhile in terms of time saved.

Beaches & Fun Parks

Children are Welcome

The Balinese are warmly affectionate and positive about children, and travelers should experience no problems taking them into restaurants or bars. Kuta now has its share of franchised fast-food places serving burgers and chips and, although children's menus are unusual, there is generally always something for them, chicken perhaps, on menus. All the better hotels have swimming pools and the upmarket resort hotels nearly all have a shallow pool for children.

Beaches

Kuta Beach

Every year there are tragic drownings off Kuta Beach because overambitious surfers and swimmers underestimate the power of the waves. However, if you stick to the designated areas between the flags there is no need to worry and children under supervision will enjoy the sea and sand. Kuta is home to Bali's biggest beach resort, with a strong Australian bias, and the white-sand beach stretches for 10km.

Sanur Beach

Many visitors consider Sanur beach to be the best on Bali. The shore stretches for about 4.5km but the best sand is to be found in the northern part near the Grand Bali Beach Hotel. Older children will love the variety of watersports that are available, including windsurfing, parasailing, jet-skiing and canoeing, and equipment may be hired on the beach or from most of the larger hotels that front the sea. It is sometimes difficult to find shady places on the beach.

Snorkeling

Children, under the super-vision of an accompanying adult in the water, will be enthralled by the experience of snorkeling, and the reefs surrounding Bali and Lombok offer superb opportunities. The inexperienced should begin by snorkeling off a beach area in shallow water. Worth considering for older children is a PADI-certified diving course. There are

diving centers in Kuta, Sanur, Lovina and Candi Dasa in Bali, and Senggigi in Lombok.

✉ **Lovina and Candi Dasa in Bali and the Gili Islands off Lombok are the best places for inexperienced snorkelers.**

Fun Parks

Adrenalin Park

The young may prefer just to watch but older children may be tempted by The Slingshot which propels two passengers, in one capsule, over 50m in two seconds. If you are really unlucky they will be tempted to try the 50m bungee jump from a purpose-built tower. There is also an artificial rock face for climbing under the supervision of qualified instructors.

✉ **69 Jalan Benasari, Kuta**
☎ **0361-757841**

Waterbom Park

A recreational complex for all the family with water rides and swimming pools. Race tracks that begin at the top of a 16m tower and shoot riders down at speeds of up to 50kph (getting airborne for a moment or two!) will appeal to reckless youngsters. Positively relaxing by comparison are the jungle rides and the river rides in tube rafts. The slides appeal to younger children. Your own food and drinks need to be smuggled in, but there are restaurants inside this beautifully landscaped complex.

✉ **Jalan Kartika Plaza, Tuban**
☎ **0361-755676** 🕐 **9–6**

Culture & Wildlife

Culture

Music

Children may enjoy sitting as close as possible to a gamelan (orchestra – ➤ 112) because this gives an opportunity to admire the skill of the musicians who perform at breakneck speed. Young children, on the other hand, may be disconcerted by being too close to the jangling noise of so many percussion instruments.

Shadow Puppet Drama

Children enjoy the novelty of a shadow puppet performance (*wayang kulit* ➤ 112), the pure skill of the one-man show and the surprising theatricality that a good puppetmaster can create. The narratives are usually drawn from Hindu epics so brush up on your knowledge of the *Ramayana* and *Mahabharata* epics. Performances usually take place at night. Ask at your hotel.

Traditional Dances

For children, some of the traditional dances are more suitable than others. The *legong* should be avoided because its refined style lacks the kind of drama that children respond to. The *Barong and Rangda* dance is basically an encounter between good and evil and the basic plot is easy to follow. Very young children may find the costume and appearance of the evil Rangda a little frightening if sitting too close to the stage. The *Sanghyang Jaran* dance is popularly advertised as the 'Fire Dance' and, as it features men dancing through a fire of coconut husks using a wooden hobbyhorse, it should engage the attention of children.

✉ **Dances are advertised everywhere in Kuta and Ubud and take place every night of the week**

Wildlife

Taman Nasional Bali Barat

The tigers are long gone, but in West Bali National Park today there are long-tailed macaque monkeys, barking and sanbar deer, and the very rare Bali starling (➤ 12, 13, 56).

Dolphin Trips from Lovina

A 6AM start to see dolphins at play off the northern coast is easily arranged in Lovina. Travelers have conflicting opinions about the worth of this exercise but children should enjoy the spectacle.

✉ **All hotels around Lovina will arrange a trip**

Taman Burung

Bali Bird Park (Taman Burung) is home to over 150 species of birds, and over a thousand animals in all, some of which are seldom seen outside Indonesia. Star attractions include resplendent birds of paradise from Irian Jaya and Komodo dragons. The 12m-high walk-in aviary is impressive and children may like the idea of breakfasting with the cockatoos or photo opportunities with some of the birds.

✉ **Jalan Serma Cok Ngurah Gambir, Singapadu (just north of Batubulan)** 🕐 **Daily 9–6** ☎ **0361-299352**

Babies

Disposable nappies are available in the supermarkets of Kuta and Sanur, as well as Ubud, but they cost more than at home. It helps to bring as many necessary items as possible in your luggage, especially wipes. Up-market hotels can generally arrange babysitters. Restaurants are happy to boil water for bottles, but it is best to always use bottled water. Remind youngsters never to drink tap water.

Traditional Dances & Music

Dances in Ubud
The very best place to enjoy an authentic dance performance is around Ubud (especially at Puri Saren Agung ➤ 55). There is a schedule with three or four different dances each night of the week and tickets can be purchased at the tourist office (☎ 0361-973285). Seats cannot be reserved so turn up early for a front-row view. Photography is allowed. Dances usually have a fixed admission rate but a transport charge is added if the venue is not within walking distance.

Dances

Different traditional dances take place regularly in southern Bali and in Ubud and at least one performance should be seen.

✉ **Ubud, Batubulan, Sanur, Nusa Dua, Denpasar. Tickets purchased in advance or at the door. Some restaurants include a dance performance before dinner.**

The *Kecak*
The 'monkey dance' is one of the more famous dances, its onomatopoeic name coming from the 'cak cak cak' chattering noise made by the chorus. The tale, from the *Ramayana*, tells of Prince Rama and his monkey army attempting to rescue his wife Sita from the clutches of the evil Ravana. The dance is dramatic, fast and musically arresting.

The *Barong and Rangda*
This dance enacts a struggle between the fun-loving Barong and the evil witch Rangda. It is one of the more enjoyable dances and usually includes a scene where the witch uses magic to force her adversaries to stab themselves with their own knives. The spell-binding costumes are invariably magnificent. In Ubud, the *calonarang* is an embroidered version of this dance with a witch queen, Calonarang, furious because no one will marry her daughter.

The *Sanghyang Jaran*
This trance dance tends to be advertised as the 'Fire Dance' because, in one version, participants dance over burning coconut husks.

The *Legong*
The *legong*, while lacking the narrative drama of other dances, is nevertheless highly refined and elegant. The kidnapped-princess-in-distress plot plays second fiddle to the courtly, intricate movements of the young girls who perform the dances.

The *Baris*
This is a warrior dance usually performed by men, either solo or in a small group, expressing the various emotions of the knightly combatant as he prepares for a battle.

Music

Gamelan
Gamelan (orchestra) music is loud and brazen but also highly structured and requiring speed of execution. Try to see the unique all-women gamelan in Ubud, which performs every Sunday evening.

✉ **Jalan Puri Peliatan, Peliatan, Ubud** ☎ **0361-973285**

Shadow Puppet Drama
A *wayang kulit* (shadow puppet) performance consists of a small orchestra, about 100 puppets, and the *dalang* (puppet-master). The puppets are made from water-buffalo hide. Even if you do not understand the Indonesian language, *wayang kulit* can be enjoyed and appreciated through the music and the skill of the *dalang* in manipulating the puppets and adopting changes of voice.

✉ **Okra Kartini in Ubud** ☎ **0361-973285** 🕐 **Sun & Wed at 8PM**

Sports

Bali and Lombok

Scuba Diving
Bali and Lombok are inexpensive places to complete a certified diving course and gain a life-long PADI (Professional Association of Diving Instructors) certificate. The best dive sites are away from the busy tourist areas and require a boat trip. Kuta, Sanur, Lovina and Candi Dasa in Bali all have well-established diving operators. Senggigi in Lombok and the Gili Islands also have operators. Some companies will be more professional than others, so shop around and ask lots of questions.

Surfing
Bali is one of the world's great surfing destinations and aficionados wax lyrical about the perfect 'tubes' they have experienced. All the necessary equipment can be bought in Kuta, or bring your own board, helmet and reef shoes. The best surfing spots are Kuta, Nusa Dua, Nusa Lembongan and, for the more experienced surfer, Uluwatu. Inexperienced surfers should keep strictly within the designated area on Kuta beach because there are frequent fatalities, many caused by the strong under-currents.
Cheyne Horan School of Surf
☎ 0361-756735

South and Southeast Bali

Bali International Rafting
This company organizes adventure rafting trips down a 12km stretch of the River Telaga Waja, in the southeast of Bali, north of Klungkung. The rafting lasts about two hours and the package trip includes transport and lunch.
✉ 7 Jalan By Pass Ngurah Rai, Sanur ☎ 0361-281408

Bungee Jumping
There are at least four companies in Bali offering a leap of faith and a guaranteed rush of adrenalin. They can be relied on for professional equipment. The Bali Bungy Co (► 58) arranges free transport within the Kuta, Sanur and Nusa Dua area and a free T-shirt and certificate awaits those who live to tell the tale!
Bali Bungy Co ☎ 0361-752658/755425
Adrenalin Park
☎ 0361-757841

Sobek
Sobek is an adventure tour company specializing in whitewater rafting trips on the River Ayung, jungle treks, sea-kayaking, bird-watching expeditions, and a spectacular descent of Gunung Batur on a bicycle.
✉ 9 Jalan Tirta Ening, By Pass Ngurah Rai, Sanur ☎ 0361-287059

Central and West Bali

Bali Adventure Tours
Well-organized kayaking, mountain biking, adventure rafting on the River Ayung, and jungle treks. Package trips include transport, equipment, lunch, insurance and qualified instructors.
✉ Adventure House, Jalan By Pass Ngurah Rai, Pesanggaran, or at Yanies restaurant (► 93)
☎ 0361-721480

Snorkeling
Bali and Lombok are both surrounded by reefs, which makes snorkeling one of the best forms of free entertainment on the islands. Bring your own gear or hire it on the beach at Sanur in southern Bali, Candi Dasa in southeastern Bali, Lovina in northern Bali, or the Gili Islands off Lombok.

Bars, Pubs & Nightclubs

Peanuts Pub Crawl

Book ahead for a place in Kuta's infamous and oversubscribed pub crawl. Every Tuesday and Saturday it starts at 6:30PM and a bus carts the increasingly inebriated group from one drinking hole to another. The opening venue is the Casablanca bar, then the two Peanuts bars, then…

☎ 0361-754149

South and Southeast Bali

Bukit Peninsula

Indian Ocean Cave Night

The Bali Cliff hotel (➤ 92 The Ocean) organizes a fairly expensive beach event on Saturdays at 7PM, starting with cocktails and followed by a barbecue buffet and *kecak* dance.

✉ Bali Cliff Hotel
☎ 0361-771992 (ext 890)

Candi Dasa

Candy Agung

At the west end of Candi Dasa, on the main road, this restaurant hosts a *legong* dance to accompany the set three-course dinner each evening. The food is Balinese and European. The formal *legong* seems an appropriate choice in this setting.

✉ Jalan Raya, Candi Dasa

Legend Rock Café

Live music on the stage each evening in a convivial pub atmosphere. Curries and pizzas served throughout the evening and an impressive drinks menu lists all the cocktails you can think of. Easy to find along the main road in Candi Dasa.

✉ Jalan Raya, Candi Dasa

Kuta

'A' Bar

A vodka bar fueled by Absolut and a hip place for a late night. Excellent cocktails, friendly staff and a lively atmosphere make it a great meeting point for those planning a very late night.

✉ Jalan Dyana Pura, Seminyak

The Bounty

This extraordinary building replicates Captain Bligh's ship, and is appropriately complemented by bar crew in naval uniforms. Happy hours are 6–8PM and 10PM–12AM with dancing from around 10PM. Leave by 2AM or walk the plank!

✉ Jalan Legian, Kuta
☎ 0361-758646

Casablanca Bar

There is a pool table, music and food in the Casablanca, a popular bar and meeting place. The infamous Peanuts Pub Crawl (➤ panel) takes over the place twice a week, but the atmosphere is always animated.

✉ 14 Jalan Buri Sari, Kuta
☎ 0361-751333

Double 6

Bali's liveliest disco, open until early morning. It has a large, open dance floor with DJs playing the latest records for a young and hip crowd. The superb location is right by the beach.

✉ Jalan Double 6,
☎ 0361-731144

Hard Rock Café

Part of the famous international chain, this brand new venue has pride of place on the Kuta beach strip. Live bands and a dance floor surrounded by the usual rock paraphernalia help create a fun atmosphere.

✉ 204 Jalan Pantai, Kuta
☎ 0361-755661

Peanuts Club

One of the more popular nightclubs in Kuta. Air-conditioned with a large dance floor, DJ and music, pool tables and karaoke bar.

Opens at 9PM; free entry before midnight.

✉ **Corner of Jalan Melasti and Jalan Legian** ☎ 0361-754149

Nusa Dua

Quinn's
Dance the night away with music from a live band or just sit and enjoy the scene in air-conditioned comfort.

✉ **Sheraton Laguna, Nusa Dua** ☎ 0361-71906

Central and West Bali

Ubud

Café Arma
This Italian restaurant (▶ 58), delightfully situated in a rural setting, has live music various nights of the week.

✉ **Jalan Hanoman** ☎ 0361-975742

Casa Luna
This pleasantly cultured restaurant (▶ 95) occasionally arranges evenings of live traditional music; check the pavement notice board.

✉ **Jalan Raya** ☎ 0361-973283 ⊕ 8–10

Putra Bar & Restaurant
A wide-screen movie at 7PM followed by live music at 9PM for a two-hour performance. An inexpensive set three-course meal is available but not obligatory. The bar opens at 5PM.

✉ **Jalan Monkey Forest, Ubud** ☎ 0361-975570

Sai Sai
A wide-screen movie is shown each evening at 7PM

and after this a group of musicians performs a jam session. This is as boisterous as it gets in sedate Ubud. The bar is easily found halfway down Jalan Monkey Forest, just past the playing fields.

✉ **Jalan Monkey Forest, Ubud** ☎ 0361-976698

North and East Bali

Lovina

Malibu
Nightlife around Lovina is very low-key and there are no discos or nightclubs. A few restaurants, and especially the Malibu restaurant (▶ 98), organize evenings of live music. The restaurant at the Rambutan Beach Cottages (▶ 103) is also worth checking out for the occasional Balinese dance show accompanying dinner.

✉ **Kalibukbuk** ☎ 0362-41671 ⊕ 8–1

Lombok

Senggigi

The Pub Downstairs
Nightlife in Lombok is restricted to the few bars in Senggigi and on Gili Trawangan. The Pub Down-stairs, below the Princess of Lombok restaurant (▶ 99), has a pool table, darts and wide-screen video but that's about it. Occasionally, some of the other restaurants have an evening of live music or even a traditional Sasak dance.

✉ **Jalan Raya, Senggigi** ☎ 0370-693011

Bars
The bars and pubs in Kuta are unlike anywhere else in Bali or Lombok. At their best they are lively and amusing and provide a good night's entertainment; at their worst, they are loud and rowdy and not to everyone's taste. In Ubud, by comparison, they are sedate and in Candi Dasa and Lovina they occasionally burst into life but are usually fairly tranquil establishments.

What's On When

Bamboo Poles and *Banten*

A sure sign of a festival or ceremony taking place in Bali are tall bamboo poles arching over the road leading into a village and brightly decorated with patterns made from the yellow leaf of coconut trees. Even more dramatic are the stunning pyramids of fruit and flowers – known as *banten* – that the women balance on their heads as they solemnly make their way to the village temple. The *banten* are offerings from the villagers to their gods and are often left overnight in the temple before being taken apart the next day.

Public Holidays

Only a few special days occur at the same time each year in Bali and Lombok and these include New Year's Day, Christmas Day and 17 August (Independence Day). The times of the most interesting holidays vary because they are calculated according to Balinese and Muslim lunar calendars.

Hindu New Year

The Hindu calendar calculates the beginning of the New Year (*Nyepi*) to be around the beginning of April or late March and the days before this are characterized by processions from temples and ceremonies to expel evil spirits. The night before *Nyepi* everyone bangs gongs, blows whistles and makes as much noise as possible to scare away the evil spirits for another year.

Muslim New Year and Ramadan

The Muslim New Year usually occurs in June or July although, from a Lombok visitor's point of view, the Ramadan month of fasting that takes place around late January and early February is more significant. Ramadan is the ninth month of the Muslim year, and strict fasting is observed from sunrise to sunset. Most restaurants outside of Senggigi will close between dawn and dusk.

Odalan Festivals

Every temple in Bali has its own *odalan* (birthday festival) and there will be other occasions that call for village festivities based around the temple. The highlight is usually the joyful afternoon procession of female villagers to the temple carrying their offerings. In the outer courtyard there will be a gamelan orchestra, dances perhaps or a shadow play (*wayang kulit* performance ► 112). Visitors are welcome to attend and unobtrusive photography is permitted. The Tourist Board issues a free calendar (► below) each year listing the dates of *odalan* festivals, which vary from year to year.

Finding a Festival

A comprehensive calendar of festivals and special events is available from the government tourist offices in Kuta, Ubud or Singaraja, and the free tourist newspapers will also carry details of forthcoming events. The tourist office in Ampenan, on Lombok, also issues a calendar of events covering Balinese and Sasak festivals and events around the island. If you stay for more than a week you should find at least one opportunity to observe and enjoy a Balinese festival, for it will prove to be a highlight of your visit.

Practical Matters

Above: *Balinese cloth*
Right: *monkeys are highly
regarded in Bali because
of their association in
Hinduism with Hanuman,
the monkey god*

117

WHAT YOU NEED

	UK	Germany	USA	Netherlands	Spain
● Required					
○ Suggested					
▲ Not required					
Passport	●	●	●	●	●
Visa	▲	▲	▲	▲	▲
Onward or return ticket	●	●	●	●	●
Inoculations (Y fever, smallpox, typhoid, cholera, hepatitis A & B , malaria)	○	○	○	○	○
Health documentation (► 123, Health)	○	○	○	○	○
Travel insurance	○	○	○	○	○
Driver's licence (international)	●	●	●	●	●
Car insurance certificate (if own car)	●	●	●	●	●
Car registration document (if own car)	●	●	●	●	●

WHEN TO GO

Bali (coastal): highland temperatures may be cooler

▓▓▓▓▓▓ High season

▢▢▢▢▢▢ Low season

30°C	30°C	30°C	30°C	30°C	28°C	28°C	28°C	30°C	30°C	30°C	30°C
JAN	FEB	MAR	APR	MAY	JUN	JUL	AUG	SEP	OCT	NOV	DEC

Very wet   Wet   Sun   Sunshine & showers

TOURIST OFFICES

In the UK (for UK, Ireland, Benelux and Scandinavia)
Indonesia Tourist
Promotion Office,
3–4 Hanover Street,
London W1 9HH
☎ (020) 7493 0030
Fax: (020) 7493 1747

In the USA
Indonesia Tourist
Promotion Office,
3457 Wilshire Boulevard,
Los Angeles, CA90010
☎ 213/387 2078
Fax: 213/380 4876

**In Germany
(for rest of Europe)**
Indonesia Tourist
Promotion Office,
Wiessenhutten Strasse, 17
D6000, Frankfurt-am-Main
☎ (069) 233677/233678

ARRIVING

The national airline, Garuda Indonesia, flies directly to Bali from Paris, Amsterdam and Vienna (in Europe) and Los Angeles (USA). Garuda Indonesia and other airlines also fly to Jakarta where you can transfer to a domestic flight for Bali or Lombok.

Ngurah Rai Airport, Bali
Km to centre of Kuta

3 kilometers

Journey times

🚌	N/A
🚐	10 minutes
🚗	10 minutes

Selaparang Airport, Lombok
Km to centre of Senggigi

10 kilometers

Journey times

🚌	N/A
🚐	30 minutes
🚗	30 minutes

MONEY

The monetary unit of Bali and Lombok is the Indonesian rupiah (Rp). There are coins of 25, 50, 100 and 500 rupiah. Notes are in denominations of 100, 500, 1,000, 5,000, 10,000, 20,000 and 50,000 rupiah. It is an idea to carry smaller denominations (50 and 100 rupiah) as taxi drivers and small stores may not have small change. Travelers' checks can be cashed at hotels, banks and money changers. Credit cards are widely accepted in popular tourist resorts on Bali.

TIME

Bali and Lombok operate on Central Indonesia Standard Time, which is eight hours ahead of Greenwich Mean Time (GMT +8).

CUSTOMS

 YES

There are specific allowances of alcohol, cigarettes and luxury goods into the country for those over 16 years of age.

Alcohol:	2 litres
Cigarettes:	200
Cigars:	50 or
Tobacco:	100 grams
Perfume:	reasonable amount
Toilet water:	reasonable amount

Cameras and other photographic (including video) equipment, radios and typewriters should be declared and recorded in your passport. These must be taken back out on your departure.

 NO

Narcotics, guns and ammunition, TV sets, radio cassette recorders, Chinese medicines. The import or export of large amounts of Indonesian currency is prohibited.

TOURIST OFFICES

Bali Government Tourism Office
● Jalan Surpati Parman
   Niti Mandala
   Renon, Denpasar
   ☎ (0361) 222387

Bali Government Tourism Office (Department of Tourism, Post and Telecommunications)
● Jalan Raya Puputan
   Niti Mandala
   Renon, Denpasar
   ☎ (0361) 225649

Badung (South Bali) Government Tourism Information Centre
● Jalan Bakung Sari
   Kuta, Denpasar
   ☎ (0361) 251419

Denpasar Government Tourism Office
● Jalan Surpati
   Denpasar
   ☎ (0361) 223602

Ngurah Rai Int Airport
● Tuban, Denpasar
   ☎ (0361) 51011

Kuta Art Market
● Jalan Bakung Sari
   Kuta, Denpasar

Bina Wisata Ubud
● Gianyar (next to village
   head's office of Ubud)

Lombok (West Nusa Tenggara Tourist Office)
● Jalan Langko 70
   Ampenan
   ☎ (0370) 31730

NATIONAL HOLIDAYS

J	F	M	A	M	J	J	A	S	O	N	D
(2)	(1)	(2)	(3)	1			2		1		1

1 Jan	New Year's Day
Jan/Feb	Chinese New Year
Mar/Apr	Balinese New Year (*Nyepi*)
Mar/Apr	Good Friday
21 Apr	Kartini Day
May	Ascension Day
15 Aug	Assumption Day
17 Aug	Independence Day (*Proklomasi Kemerdekaan*)
5 Oct	Armed Forces Day
25 Dec	Christmas Day

Other holidays have dates that, being based on calendars other than the Western (Gregorian) calendar, change significantly every year. Check with a Balinese calendar during your visit.

OPENING HOURS

○ Shops	● Museums
● Offices	○ Post Offices
● Banks	○ Pharmacies (*apotiki*)

8AM	9AM	10AM	11AM	NOON	2PM	4PM	6PM	8PM

☐ Day	☐ Midday
☐ Evening	

In addition to the times in the chart, some shops do not close for lunch, but remain open through the day. Most shops are open Saturday and some also open Sunday. Offices close at 11AM Friday and 12.30PM Saturday. Banks close at 11AM Saturday and are shut Sunday. Banks in hotels open longer hours. Money changers are generally open until the evening.

Museum opening times vary (see individual museums in the 'What to See' section).

Most pharmacies open on Saturday. On Sundays they open on a rotation basis.

PUBLIC TRANSPORT

 Inter-island Flights There are regular daily flights between Bali (Denpasar) and Lombok (Mataram). Flight time is 25 minutes. Services are operated by Garuda-Merpati (Bali ☎ 0361 222864; Lombok ☎ 0370 32226). There are also flights from Bali and Lombok to Sumbawa, a small island east of Lombok. The planes are quite small so book early.

 Buses On Bali buses cover the main 'inter-town' routes, with Denpasar as the central terminal. In addition, all main routes, as well as minor passable ones, are covered by *bemos* (minibuses) – sometimes called 'colts' after the Mitsubishi Colt. On Lombok public buses and *bemos* cover the main routes. Off the main routes you may be restricted to a pony cart (*cidemo*).

 Ferries There is a regular 24-hour car ferry service between Bali (Padangbai) and Lombok (Lembar). The trip takes at least four hours, sometimes up to seven hours. Alternatively, there is the faster, jet-powered catamaran, the *Mabua Express*, from Bali's Benoa Harbour to Lembar. The trip takes two hours but is more expensive than the ferry (information: Bali ☎ 0361 721212; Lombok ☎ 0370 681195).

 Urban Transport In Denpasar, *bemos* (see Buses, above) skirt the central area, going between the various bus/bemo terminals and to other points around the city. In the city center, three-wheeled mini-*bemos* (*tiga rodas*) are the main mode of transport; you find them lined up at each of the terminals (a letter on the back indicates their route). This is the main form of transport for other towns.

CAR RENTAL

 On Bali and Lombok local operators are cheaper than big international operators. An International driving permit is needed. You may need a licence and to leave your passport as security; check insurance cover. A wide range of vehicles is available.

TAXIS

 Blue and yellow (air-conditioned) taxis are becoming more common in Denpasar and some tourist areas of Bali, but do not use one whose meter 'isn't working'. For taxis from the airport pay at the counter prior to your journey. Refuse offers from touts at the airport.

DRIVING

 There is a two-lane motorway between Denpasar and Benoa. Speed limit: **96kph.**

 Speed limit on all country roads: **96kph**

 Speed limit on urban roads: **48kph**

 Seat Belts No laws at present.

 Breath Testing There are no laws, but avoid alcohol when driving.

 Petrol (*bensin*) is sold by the government-owned Pertamina company and is reasonably cheap. You will find petrol stations in every large town, however in rural areas they are few and far between – when you see one, fill up. In an emergency there are roadside shops selling fuel from a drum, but this will be more expensive.

 With the exception of the Denpasar–Benoa motorway, most roads are badly pot-holed or are tracks. Punctures are a common occurrence; fortunately you will rarely be far from someone who can fix it for you (look for signs: 'Presban', 'Servis' or 'Bengkel'). Check your car for a spare tyre before driving it away. Contact the hire company for any other breakdown.

PERSONAL SAFETY

Crime against the person is rare in Bali and Lombok but you should guard belongings against theft. On Bali the Lake Batur area is crime-prone and the Kintamani-Bangli region is dubious. Items are rarely recovered.

To help prevent crime:

- Avoid walking after dark.
- Beware if you travel on local buses/*bemos*.
- Do not leave possessions unattended anywhere.
- Never carry your passport, airline ticket or more money than you need.
- Lombok is a Muslim island, exposing flesh is offensive.

Police assistance:
☎ **110**
from any call box

TELEPHONES

Bali and Lombok's telephone service is operated by Telekom. There are several types of public phone, some allow international calls and some take phone cards (*kartu telepon*). You can also use Telekom offices (*kantor telekomunikasi*), usually called *wartels*, where you pay at the desk at the end of your call.

International Dialing Codes	
From Bali to:	
UK:	**001 44**
Germany:	**001 49**
USA:	**001 1**
Netherlands:	**001 31**
Spain:	**001 34**

POST

Post Offices
Many hotels provide postal services, or there is a post office in every major town and village. In Denpasar the main post office is at Jalan Raya Puputan, Renon ☎ (0361) 223568.
On Lombok: Jalan Langko, Mataram.
Open: 8AM–2PM (8AM–noon Fri, 1PM Sat). Closed Sun.

ELECTRICITY

The power supply in most hotels is:
220 volts, 50 cycles AC (some districts still 110 volts).

 Sockets accept two-round-pin-style plugs.

Electrical appliances without dual voltage may require a voltage transformer.
For most Western visitors, an electrical adaptor is needed.

TIPS/GRATUITIES

Yes ✓   No ✕

Tipping is not normal practice on Bali or Lombok. Do not insist on giving anyone a tip as many islanders look on tipping as charity and find it humiliating.

Hotels (if service not included)	✓	10–15%
Restaurants (if service not included)	✓	10–15%
Bar service	✓	10%
Taxis (negotiate price first, tip optional)	✓	10–15%
Tour guides	✓	change
Porters	✓	Rp1,000
Hairdressers	✓	Rp1,000

Insurance
Medical insurance is essential, including provision to get 'medi-vacced' by air-ambulance if necessary. Specialist facilities are very limited; basic medical treatment is not too expensive.

Dental Services
Have a thorough dental check-up before leaving home. It is not hard to find a dentist (*doktor gigi*) on Bali; in Denpasar there is Dr Indra Guizot, 19 Jalan Pattimura (☎ 0361 226455).

Sun Advice
Bali and Lombok are close to the equator and the sun is immediately overhead all year round. It is easy to burn, even in the shade. Always wear a hat and sunglasses, drink plenty of fluids and use a high-protection sunblock.

Drugs
Most drugs, analgesics, antibiotics etc can be obtained at pharmacies (*apotiki*) without prescription. Anti-malaria tablets should be taken before, during, and after your visit to Lombok (Bali is malaria-free). Take a small medical kit from home.

Safe Water
It is not safe to drink unboiled tap water. Good, cheap bottled water (especially the 'Aqua' brand) is sold everywhere. Most ice is made with purified water but can be risky. Salads washed in local water are best avoided.

CONCESSIONS

Students/Youths: Bali and Lombok are ideal for youth travel. They offer bargain-priced adventure. Bali in particular is geared to young visitors and many find the surf, shops and bars in Kuta ideal. Your money will go further if you rent a room without air-conditioning, and you can get a cheap, filling meal from a *warung* (food stall). The International Student Identity Card (ISIC) is worth bringing as it is recognized by many establishments.

Senior Citizens: Bali and Lombok are not suitable for elderly tourists unless they are especially fit and can cope with the heat. The rough roads and temple stairways are very taxing.

CLOTHING SIZES

NB
In Bali and Lombok
S = Small
M = Medium
L = Large

Bali and Lombok	UK	Rest of Europe	USA	
36	36	46	36	**Suits**
38	38	48	38	
40	40	50	40	
42	42	52	42	
44	44	54	44	
46	46	56	46	
7	7	41	8	**Shoes**
7.5	7.5	42	8.5	
8.5	8.5	43	9.5	
9.5	9.5	44	10.5	
10.5	10.5	45	11.5	
11	11	46	12	
S	14.5	37	14.5	**Shirts**
S	15	38	15	
M	15.5	39/40	15.5	
M	16	41	16	
L	16.5	42	16.5	
L	17	43	17	
S	8	34	6	**Dresses**
S	10	36	8	
M	12	38	10	
M	14	40	12	
L	16	42	14	
L	18	44	16	
4.5	4.5	37.5	6	**Shoes**
5	5	38	6.5	
5.5	5.5	38.5	7	
6	6	39	7.5	
6.5	6.5	40	8	
7	7	41	8.5	

LANGUAGE

Bahasa Indonesia (literally 'Indonesian language') is the national language of Indonesia, but, although it is widely used on Bali and Lombok, the local language is Balinese, or Bahasa Bali, which is altogether different with a different vocabulary. It is a very difficult language for a foreigner to get to grips with; for that reason it is best to use Bahasa Indonesia if you want to communicate with locals on Bali or Lombok. Indonesian is fairly easy to learn as there are no tenses, no genders and often one word can convey the meaning of a whole sentence. In any case, many islanders speak English, particularly in major tourist centers.

Guesthouse, small hotel	*losmen*	soap	*sabun*
room	*kamar*	one night	*satu malam*
bed	*tempat tidur*	how much? (money)	*Berapa? (harga)*
toilet (WC)	*way say*	one person	*satu orang*
bathroom	*kamar mandi*	another, one more	*satu lagi*
boiled water	*air puti*	no/not/negative	*tidak/bukan*
		sleep	*tidur*

bank	*bank*	very	*sekali*
post office	*kantor pos*	expensive	*mahal*
How much?	*Berapa?*	one	*satu*
money	*harga*	two	*dua*
ticket	*karcis*	a half	*setenga*, pronounced 'stenga'

restaurant	*rumah makan*	rice	*nasi*
food	*makan*	potatoes	*kentang*
tea	*teh*	(fried/chips)	*(goreng)*
coffee (with milk)	*kopi (susu)*	vegetable salad	
beer	*bir*	(cooked)	*gado-gado*
water (drinking)	*air (minum)*	chicken	*ayam*
May we have our bill please?	*Coba berikan rekening saya?*	hot	*panas*
		cold	*dingin*
bread	*roti*	pineapple	*nanas*
fish	*ikan*	bananas	*pisanv*

bus	*bis*	I want to go to...	*Saya mau ke...*
ship	*kapal*	Where?	*Dimana?*
motorcycle	*sepeda motor*	Which way?	*Kemana?*
bicycle	*sepeda*	What time?	*Jam berapa?*
stop	*berhenti*	Where is..?	*Dimana ada..?*
village	*desa*	near	*dekat*

Good morning	*Selamat pagi*	Goodbye	*selamat tinggal*
Good day	*selamat siang*	Help!	*Tolong!*
no/not/negative	*tidak/bukan*	Call a doctor!	*Panggil dokter!*
Thank you	*terima kasih*	Call an ambulance	*Ambulin*
Please	*silakan*	My name is...	*Nama saya...*
sorry	*ma'af*	tomorrow/ yesterday	*besok/kemarin*
good, fine, OK	*baik*	I don't understand	*Saya tidak mengerti*

124

INDEX

Acknowledgments
The Automobile Association and Periplus Editions wish to thank the following libraries, photographers and associations for their assistance in the preparation of this book:

KONINKLIJK INSTITUUT VOOR DE TROPEN 11b, 11c
MRI BANKERS' GUIDE TO FOREIGN CURRENCY 119
A J WALKER 122a, 122b
Cover photographs: STEVE VIDLER/PHOTOBANK SINGAPORE, main photo; LUCA TETTONI/ PHOTOBANK SINGAPORE, top and bottom insets

The remaining pictures are from the Association's own library (AA PHOTO LIBRARY) and were taken by JIM HOLMES with the exception of the following:

D BUWALDA 2, 5a, 6b, 7b, 8c, 9c, 12a, 12/13, 14a, 18/19, 21b, 26b, 33b, 34b, 35b, 56, 60b, 61, 70b, 84, 86b, 91a, 91b, 92/116, 117b, 122c
B DAVIES 1, 8b, 9b, 10, 14b, 15a, 16a, 17a, 18a, 18b, 19a, 20a, 21a, 22a, 22b, 23a, 23b, 24a, 24b, 25a, 25b, 26a, 27b, 28/9, 36, 44b, 57, 63, 66, 77b, 78, 82, 85b, 87, 90b

Author's Acknowledgements
Sean Sheehan would like to thank the many kind people in Bali and Lombok who assisted him with the research of this book.

Contributors
Page Layout: Design 23 Verifier: Polly Phillimore Researchers (Practical Matters): Colin Follett and Lesley Allard Indexer: Marie Lorimer 2001 edition updated by: Richard Watson